Inspired Selling

Inspired Selling

Experiential Teaching of Leadership Selling

Tips for Leading Customers to Ever-Increasing Success

Brian A Mitchell

ISBN: 1517523680
ISBN 13: 9781517523688
Library of Congress Control Number: 2015916435
CreateSpace Independent Publishing Platform
North Charleston, South Carolina

Table of Contents

Acknowledgments

I am not alone, and I didn't become who I am by myself. As I write this sales handbook, I have much for which to be grateful and many people to acknowledge. My life experiences, combined with business stints with small start-ups, giant corporations, and others in between have given me a wealth of valuable learning. My formal, informal, circumstantial, and experiential training have contributed generously to my humble toolkit.

My life story is rich with variety, adversity, and opportunity. Socrates wrote, "The unaware life is not worth living." I don't completely agree with that assertion because all life is worth living, but it surely makes sense to contend that being unaware of who you are in life will diminish your opportunities of living life to the fullest. Growing up, I was one of thirteen children. My parents were uneducated, and we happened to be very poor. I had to work really hard to get out of the reality that was handed to me in order to create a new reality. A frightened and insecure kid, I continually had to fight fear, hurtfulness, and ignorance in order to establish a lifetime pattern of continuous improvement or work toward mastery. Self-realization has enabled me to see the incredible value of the struggles in my life and apply that value to my vision, my values, and my life's mission.

I have often been tempted to bemoan and begrudge my earlier life and wish that I could have taken another route to get me to where I am. After extensive consideration and enlightenment, I have come to accept my education as unconventional or other than normal but nonetheless one of significant content and preparation for the road ahead.

Such great companies as Burroughs Corporation (Unisys), Digital Equipment Corporation (HP), IDX Systems Corporation (GE), and GE Healthcare have gainfully employed me. I have also worked for a handful of very small companies, including my own independent work environment, and spent particularly valuable time with a notable small company called SPi Healthcare (Conifer Health). Each one of these has taught me something that I can use to help others.

Let me not omit that I learned "rigor" in such environments, because it was a trademark of all of my large employers. I intend to illustrate a fair amount of that rigor in the pages ahead.

The small companies brought a mix of education, success, and frustration that has been enlightening and edifying in interesting and often peculiar ways. The most fun and possibly the greatest growth that I have experienced was in a start-up operation that mistakenly went public too early, in my opinion, and eventually failed. The excitement and passion that I had for the business and my personal success within it were quite amazing, but sadly the company ultimately filed for bankruptcy. That was the only time that a position of mine was terminated; the layoff was due to the impending bankruptcy filing. I learned a great deal from the days immediately following my termination and have used that experience multiple times during my career.

I want to acknowledge these experiences as being instrumental in shaping my passion for and knowledge of the subject of sales. I also want to acknowledge my first manager, Dave Willey, as a strong influence in my early career. Dave was an old-school professional who taught me "the customer is always the customer, but the customer is not always right." His sage approach to selling and business in general was an early model that helped me begin to shape a successful sales and leadership career.

More recently, my teammates at IDX, GE, and SPi Healthcare have been and continue to be very encouraging to me as a leader. I have seen great results in their careers and have been amply rewarded by their successes.

Finally, in tempest-in-a-teapot situations and smooth sailing alike, the master of the universe provides me with inspiration, love, wisdom, guidance, peace, and contentment beyond what I can comprehend. I owe everything and surrender everything, including this writing, to him. My heart's desire to help others be successful does not derive from my own selfish nature, but from a new nature and continuous renewal from the fountain of great wisdom that he provides.

Introduction

Have you ever experienced a day that changed your life's vocational direction? Do you remember it? I have, and I do!

I remember the scene outside Professor Roberts's office just as if it were yesterday. It was final-exam time, and this instructor was making us all sell one-on-one to him as a large part of our final grade. The atmosphere was tenser than any I had ever experienced. It was almost surreal.

The course was titled Salesmanship, and it was very different from anything that I had ever been previously exposed to in school. Professor Roberts was a very high-energy former sales leader for a Fortune 500 company. He was also a pretty intense gentleman who would tolerate no student being even as little as three minutes late to class. I witnessed him kicking a student out for being late. He was one of the most demanding and challenging teachers at my school at the time. Tiny Johnson State College, not known for academic excellence in the business curriculum, had a semityrannical professor teaching business courses, demanding full-out effort, and striving for excellence in every way, all the time!

As I nervously waited my turn to go face the "monster be-hind the door," I saw more than one student come either storm-ing or cowering out of his office. Some students were in tears; others were absolutely livid. I assumed that both reactions were caused by the treatment that the students received while behind the door. Some of the verbal reactions and the scenes that I wit-nessed were very disturbing to me.

My fear and anxiety dramatically escalated as my desire to do well and my hatred of failure began to take over my mind and body. Sweat from my armpits poured down my sides. My hands were freezing from nervous energy. I felt like a basketball player standing at the free-throw line with seconds left on the clock, whose next move would mean either a win or a loss for the team—only this was much worse. In my highly stressed condition, I think my knees came close to actually knocking. It was an amaz-ing and very scary feeling. I felt like running away. I had to go in shortly and attempt this "difficult sell" on a painting contract that my imaginary company would offer my professor's imaginary con-struction project. I knew that I would have imaginary competition but had no idea how he would respond to me when I walked in. I had a confirmed appointment, but apparently that didn't matter with this imaginary prospect, as evidenced by the failures that came pouring, one after another, out of his office.

Finally, it was my turn to enter the torture chamber for the test of all tests. "Here goes nothing," I remember muttering to myself as I charged into the room.

"Good morning, Mr. Roberts!" I said with an enthusiastic smile.

"Yes, yes, what have you got for me?" he thundered.

"I am here to offer you a quality painting service and an excel-lent price with on-time completion," I said with conviction.

"You know what?" he said. "I don't have time for this!"

Whoa! What was going on? He was throwing me out. Aha, yet another flunked student to notch in his already hacked-up belt. *No way,* I thought. *I am not leaving! I can't leave! I can't fail!*

"But we have a confirmed appointment!" I said professionally but without the confidence of my initial greeting.

"I don't care! I don't have time!" he said.

Again I tried to convince him that I offered quality, price, and on-time completion and that he should listen to me. I even provided top-notch references.

His response was the same. "I just don't have time to talk to you. Now get out of here!"

Wow! Now what? My vision went blurry, and my head began to swim with thoughts. I felt frozen in the harsh reality of not knowing what to do to resurrect this lost opportunity. There no longer seemed to be any words to claim or moves to make. I was stuck in a swirl without an escape route on which to rely. Panic was setting in. Then suddenly—I don't really know how long it took to happen or how or why it happened—a light went on in my brain with regard to his prior statement.

I somehow mustered the courage and composure to say, "What if I could show you how to save time…would you talk to me then?"

"You can save me time?" he asked.

After a strange but brief pause, I said, "Yes, sir! I can work with your clients in advance to find out what they want, the colors and finishes they prefer, and the time requirements that they have…"

The rest is a fond memory. He signed the order and sent me on my way, but not without first reminding me that he told me three times that he was "short of time" before I got it. Hey, at least I got it, right? I also got an A for the exam and the course.

And most important, I began to realize that "listening to hear" was crucial. I also began to realize that some of the imaginary variables of that sales call were just that—imaginary. That will be addressed later in this handbook.

I considered that brief but difficult "sweat-equity" lesson from Professor Roberts to be sort of a kick in the butt. In hindsight, I have great respect for how he taught and consider him one of the best, if not *the* best, teachers I had during my undergraduate studies. I have received many kicks in the butt along the way, both in my personal life and my professional life. None of them ever felt like a pat on the back; they all hurt like heck. But they all were probably needed at the time and have cumulatively helped me as much as or more than any pats on the back that I ever received, although pats on the back are also important.

Years later I realized something that will always stick with me. I realized that great salespeople are *not* born but made. No matter how fortunate, beautiful, or intelligent you are, being a great or even adequate salesperson can only be accomplished with a strong desire to succeed, plenty of hard work, and a healthy respect for the profession and the people you serve—your clients. If you are not convinced in your mind and heart that you want to be a salesperson, you will almost certainly struggle in the profession. You should find something that is a better fit for you.

This handbook is written as a tribute to all who honor the sales profession and who seek to improve their service to prospects and clients. It is also written for those who are willing to change to gain a competitive edge. I consider sales to be more about business development than selling—that is, a vocation focused on helping clients to become more successful and not on trying to get them to buy something that I am selling. Therefore, this handbook really applies to all commercial endeavors and to those who provide leadership within them.

By applying leadership skills and concepts to the sales process, you can stay focused on "them" and not "you"; as such, you remain better intentioned and able to serve those to whom you "sell." As you read this handbook, I hope you become inspired to equip yourself as a leader and achieve selling excellence through leadership. I am convinced that if you embrace selling through leadership, you will change your life both professionally and personally.

One word of caution: A commercial leader and not a professional author with skillful writing techniques is completing this work. I write as I speak and may seem to be talking to you rather than writing instructional documentation. I hope you are OK with that, because what I am writing comes straight from my heart, with a few technical processes and third-party contributions sprinkled in to help clarify some of the science of selling.

Selling Is Art

Yes, selling is part art, that is, if you consider art the ability to read people, understand people, and really hear and not just listen to them, which are all aspects of personality. Can you as a salesperson survive on art alone? Perhaps for a time you can. Can you be effective over a long period of time in a complex and competitive sales environment? My opinion is that you will never reach your unique potential if you limit yourself to art.

Having a likable personality is surely a plus when selling, and you could argue that it is a key characteristic when selling professionally. After all, who wants to have to deal with a negative or difficult personality? Who wants to buy from someone who doesn't understand what the client or prospect is saying and has to be directed every step of the way?

You could argue further that things like eye contact, smiling, tone of voice, hand gestures, posture, and other physical attributes all figure in the art of selling. As a matter of practice, a professional salesperson who wants to attain greatness had best have mastered being personable and become a good hearer rather than just a listener. In other words, the professional salesperson must develop a genuine, transparent quality that makes him or her trustworthy and reliable in the eyes of the prospective client. It is really difficult to fool a buyer for very long. So, for me, becoming someone who is genuine and likeable is 90 percent of the struggle to become great at the art of selling. I use the word "struggle" literally, because becoming better at anything requires change and effort.

Expecting different results while doing the same things over and over is an unrealistic expectation. Some say that Albert Einstein and others referred to the practice as the very definition of insanity. I find that particular definition difficult to debate; you must struggle to improve if you are to attain better results. Struggling is not a bad thing; it figures in opting for truth over harmony, turning obstacles into opportunities, acting as one's brother's keeper, and finding one's unique potential, which will all be discussed later. All of these principles include struggles if they are practiced in earnest. Selling cannot be a successful art form without struggle.

The cornerstone of the art of selling is leadership itself. People define leadership in many ways. Probably by now, thousands of books have been written, courses taught, and lectures or speeches delivered that provide perspectives on leadership. I have read a number of books, attended a number of classes and seminars, listened to a number of speeches, and participated in a number of blog forums on leadership myself. In almost every opportunity, I learned something that I incorporated into my thinking, used to alter my thinking, added to my thinking, or simply disregarded as being of no value. Some viewpoints, while inspiring and exciting and fun to read or hear and stimulating to think about, did not fit with my character, skill set, or heart- and mind-set, so I could contemplate them but not use them.

In order to move smoothly, clearly, and quickly into my vision of leadership and selling through leadership, I will first explain what I mean by heart-set and mind-set. I view my role as a "helper." In the context of the art of selling, being a helper truly has to begin with more than art; it must begin with a sincere desire to help. From that root will grow the art of caring, the art of listening and hearing, and the art of being empathetic.

These characteristics are considered arts only contrast to the mechanics of selling, which I refer to as "science." The arts require intentional and focused effort; we must build habitual behavior that allows us to exhibit these traits as part of our everyday selling process. I am convinced that you can only be highly effective at the science of selling if you are also effective at the art of selling.

To heighten your awareness of the significance of the art of selling, respond to the following:

- Do you read clients as well as you would like to read them?
- Do you understand objectives as well as you would like to?
- Do you know who is making the decision in every one of your deals?
- Are you clear on who is for you or against you in any given opportunity?

These are just a few of the many difficult questions that require the fine art of selling to answer. "But what if I can't answer them?" you may ask. Then how do you become excellent at what you do?

The ability to understand is key to solving this puzzle; it provides the insight to be able to help others. Understanding the needs, thoughts, feelings, and obstacles presented by others requires getting to the truth. Desiring getting to the truth requires the heart- and mind-sets of wanting to be helpful and knowing that is best accomplished by fully understanding the real needs of the prospect.

Galileo remarked, "All truths are easy to understand once they are discovered; the point is to discover them." Galileo's quote isn't so exceptionally profound. When you discover the truth, of course you will understand it. You won't even know what you have discovered if you don't understand it, right? But first you have to find out what the truth really is. That skill is very important in the art of selling.

I have listened to many sales presentations, sat in on many sales calls, read many sales proposals, and reviewed or built many sales presentations through the years. Can you identify the most common practice undertaken in most of those situations? From my experience it was that most people preferred to tell or present to the prospective client how great they are at what they do. Sometimes they don't even get to the good reasons why the prospects should consider buying from them. If my brief assessment seems critical to you, it is because it is intended to be sharply so. Once I learned and accepted that this was the wrong approach to use, it changed my perspective completely about selling and the real purpose of it. Consequently, it also changed my approach to doing my job.

First, I will tell you why I find "presentation mode" to be ineffective. Then I will briefly explain a successful, alternative approach, thereby laying the groundwork for the remainder of this handbook.

In the late 1980s, I learned how to beat our largest competitor in businesses where my company had never before beaten them. The secret to my success was not easy to act on, but it is quite simple to explain. I used the art of selling to the clients in question, whereas the competitor was stuck in "presentation mode." My art involved learning the truth about the prospect's needs, desires, restrictions, budget, decision-making process, biases, and anything else that I could learn about them. To do so, I asked them questions, and I listened long and intentionally enough to hear what they were saying. It was a simple formula, but not an easy one. Often we sales professionals will ask questions to probe to one or two levels and then leave it at that. More often than not, additional probing questions are needed to get to the truth. You can't assume your prospect will be great communicators and teachers for your benefit. It will take two to effectively communicate, and that means deep participation on your part.

I cannot emphasize enough the importance of communicating as the way to uncovering the truth. And getting to the truth is the *only* way to really know what prospects need to make them successful. Without the truth you have only speculation or perhaps a bit of good fortune. So ask yourself, what is better—knowing the truth or sticking with speculation?

Back-to-basics thinking provides my foundation for mastering the art of selling; the root must be a desire to help others enough to radically seek to learn the truth about them and understand them. After that, you can easily position your solution for them to meet their objectives. From that root, the art of selling will branch out to all areas needed for sales excellence, which will include the science of selling.

In her book *Stop Telling, Start Selling*, Linda Richardson talks extensively about "dialogue selling" instead of "telling" prospects. She references three types of salespeople:

- Product salespeople
- Quasi-consultative salespeople
- Consultative salespeople

Most of us fall into the first two categories. The irony is that most of us think that we are in the third category. Many of us truly do attempt to dialogue with prospects, but we quickly revert to being product salespeople in the heat of battle for prospect acceptance. It requires intentional, focused effort and honest self-assessment to move up from the first to the second or the second to the third in these salesperson categories.

Don't expect to master the art of consultative selling immediately if you are not already there; old habits tend to die hard. But if you really want to become great, you will be willing to pause when objections are thrown your way by a prospect. Then, instead of selling attributes, you will ask more questions. Why should you do that? You should do that so that you can get closer to the truth. One of my first sales-training courses taught me that "smoking out" objections was critical to selling success. The way I was taught to smoke out objections is no longer a tactic that I use, but I did learn that, many times, stated objections are simply smoke screens and need to be vetted rather than automatically accepted as the truth.

Becoming a consultative salesperson, for me, amounts to simply (though not easily) seeking the truth with every ounce of energy that I can muster. And my reason for seeking the truth is that I want to help the prospect be successful, and the best way to figure out how to help them is to know the truth!

Selling Is Science

O ften, when an aspiring professional has mastered the art of selling, she or he may not have a good grasp of the science component and will still fall short of goals. I have seen this happen repeatedly; someone who is great at building relationships will have great difficulty in forecasting and closing deals. What is missing? The answer is simple—the science of selling is missing. Those of you who lack that component need a step-by-step methodology that you can follow to complete the actions necessary for getting the desired results—that is, closing the sale.

A systematic process instills both intelligence and rigor into the sales cycle. The intelligence provided through forecasting, funnel management, and the system's own rhythm establishes a better way to not only understand but also control the sales cycle. The rigor instilled by the system enables the development of positive habits that truly empower salespeople. The building of positive habits can initially involve a fair amount of work, but the payoff is that the habits become part of your behavioral DNA, that is, part of who you are and not just of what you do.

Funnel management and funnel stratification are two areas that provide the mechanism for the establishment of significant intelligence and rigor in the sales process. Understanding whether the customer can buy, if they will buy from you, and whether their timetable is matched to yours; moving and tracking the process through the various stages; and identifying the potential of the sale are all *key* components of successful selling.

These simple definitions will help you understand these two concepts better:

(a) Funnel Management—Funnel management is being able to understand and rank the probability of the prospect buying a product and also whether or not they will buy from you. Without this level of understanding, you may be wasting time trying to help a prospect who either is not in a situation to be helped or isn't interested in you being their helper. In either case, if they will not be buying from you, there are significant opportunity costs to you to initiate effort without positive results.

It is important to learn the answers to these questions:

1. When will they buy?
2. How will they go about that process?

When working with a prospective client you should be very clear with them that you can best help them if you understand what their buying timing and buying process is. With that understanding, you can appropriately synchronize providing them needed information, presentations, brain-storming sessions, or simply keeping them properly educated on what products' values are and any possible changes that occur. Since communication is so important, being right on time and providing the right information is a significant help to them and a significant advantage over the competition for you.

If the prospect's buying process is well understood, you will know not only when to provide information, but you will also know the best-suited format in which to provide the information. As an example, if they have a step in the process that includes a technical fit discussion with a small group, you need to find out who will be attending and the roles that they play, whether the format is a question-and-answer type or a more formal process requiring a presentation, how much time is allotted, and most important, what the goal(s) of the meeting are for them.

Knowing these variables will allow you to better determine your fit for the prospect. If your company typically does well in their style of process, you will have a better idea of how successful you will be. In addition, the more information the prospect is willing to provide you, the greater the odds of being a good fit for them you will become.

As a by-product of understanding these variables and your potential business fit and product fit, you will be better equipped to provide accurate forecast ranking/categorization for the prospect. If you use a ranking for business fit and potential of 1–10 with 10 being an ideal fit, the more you know, the more accurate your forecasting will be. Confidence level is reflected in ranking, but it must be based on truth and understanding and not on a hunch or what I often refer to as "fatal optimism." Fatal optimism is allowing hope to trump truth and become a costly flaw in your process.

Understanding if budget is approved and the money is earmarked for the project that you are working on is critical. If in either of these situations the answers are not affirmative, you will likely be wasting your time. Where in the buy process is the prospect?

Finding out from the prospect if your company is really a contender for the business is also important to avoiding wasting time. You won't win every deal, so win as many as you can and walk away from those that you can't win.

Funnel Stratification—Funnel stratification is the process of taking what you have learned from the prospect's buying process and applying it to the steps or stages in the "walk to close" and path to getting the buy completed for the prospect.

The three main phases of the walk to close are

1. outside the closing sales stages: early phases when you are just getting to know the prospect and they you. No decisions have yet been made, and perhaps no meetings have occurred. The prospect has been identified as intending to make a buy, but detailed due diligence has yet to occur;
2. within the range of the closing sales stages: moving the deal toward closure with meetings, proposals, estimates, and agreements;
3. within the final closing sales stages: negotiating and closing the deal.

To get to the identification of these rankings, steps, dates, and buying forecasts, you must first know the following:

- What are the goals of the buyer?
- Who is buying and what process is followed?
- Is there money to buy, and if so, how and when is it made available to the buyer?
- Who is the competition?

Then, using tools such as account or deal planners, and presentation methodologies that require prospect understanding, you not only gain additional intelligence that can be shared with your team and management, but you become able to align with customers and determine business fit with them better than your competitors will.

I once did a presentation (EDGE Power Presentation) to a prospect who informed me that he was going to buy a particular computer company's product and that he was going to buy it directly from that company. I thought the better solution for him was an alternative company's system and, of course, wanted him to buy from me. When I completed the presentation it was clear that he intended to not only buy from me, but also to buy the solution that I recommended versus the one he originally indicated that he would purchase. I had done some research ahead of time on his institution and incorporated it into the Power Presentation; my intention was to establish business fit. The customer actually learned things about his company that he was not previously aware of. And he learned that our goals were well aligned with his. He was sufficiently impressed and convinced of our fit that he trusted my team and me with not only the recommendation, but also the configuration and sale of the solution. Never underestimate the power of an effective presentation.

So how was I able to do so well with the presentation that I made to that prospect? I did my homework ahead of time. It took intentional focus, eagerness to help the prospect, and the amount of preparation that would enable me to understand the prospect as much as possible before doing the presentation. There is much more to this particular story, but the bottom line is that I used the art of selling to enable me to engage fully and effectively in the science of selling, and then I combined both arts to win over a very good client.

Some of the most successful sales companies in the world have become so because they have taught people to follow a proven process and do it over and over again. Companies such as Amway have produced many multimillionaires that were simply willing to follow the Amway sales process. They were most often very average people with a desire to be successful and the willingness to be taught, be coached, and follow a system.

I have examined several such sales processes and discovered that I am less of a scientist and more of an artist when it comes to selling. When I was eighteen years old and unable to put resources together to get into college, I sold vacuum cleaners. We were taught to use a proven method of selling that was very scientific. I soon became both very successful and very dissatisfied with the job, and I quit. Not long afterward, I sold advertising on telephone-book covers. I discovered then how to incorporate art into the scientific approach and again was very successful for a period of time before moving on.

Years later, as I examined those two experiences, I determined that I was fine with the science of selling and more than fine with the art of selling. What I was missing in both cases was the passion for selling the products that I had to sell.

Selling Is Passion

One definition of "passion" is any powerful or compelling emotion or feeling, such as love or hate. Another is a strong or extravagant fondness, enthusiasm, or desire for anything, such as *a passion for music or a passion for selling. What does that mean? Well, it could mean different things to different people, depending on which aspects of the process they are passionate about. No matter which aspect, passion is certainly an advantage in the selling process.*

PASSION FOR CHALLENGE
Some people have a passion for selling because it presents a challenge. That challenge could simply be the challenge to win, which is important, but it should not be the sole driver behind selling. Remember, selling should be about helping the customer; if winning at all cost blurs that vision, the process can become dangerous and destructive.

PASSION FOR PEOPLE
Other salespeople are primarily motivated by their love of people. Selling certainly offers opportunities to work and interact

with fellow human beings. The importance of this characteristic cannot be diminished; no matter how much a salesperson may relish the challenge of winning the deal, he or she will be less happy and less successful than another salesperson who enjoys working with people.

PASSION FOR SUCCESS

Success can be measured tangibly, but it can also be experienced intangibly. Tangible measurement is easily determined by whether quotas are met and deals are closed. Intangible measurement is much more akin to the concept that "beauty is in the eye of the beholder." Some salespeople are happy with establishing friendly relationships with clients. That is all good, but if those friendships never ring the cash register, they must be evaluated from a business perspective. Otherwise, salespeople are simply spending cycles on a personal level during business hours and not getting any closer to making their quotas. For me, a combination of a strong personal relationship and getting the lion's share of a company's business is what really defines success. It doesn't always happen, but when it does, it is magic!

PASSION FOR THE PRODUCT

I shared earlier that I was successful in two instances of selling within systems but unhappy with the jobs. The reason was that the products marginalized me, even though the systems and my passion for accomplishing something and making money sustained me for a time. In two other situations, where I found neither passion for the product nor a systematic approach to selling in place, I floundered. In each situation the product was weak to begin with, and then, when I fully discovered that my attitude was negative, the jobs headed straight for the septic tank. There was no turning back for me; I was fast-tracking to the worst sales experiences that I ever had. Those failures led to me leaving both companies and learning an incredibly valuable lesson: Don't sell it if you don't believe in it! Since then, I have considered but then declined multiple opportunities because passion just wasn't there.

If you don't have a winning attitude, you will lose. Baseball great Yogi Berra once said, "Life is like baseball. It's 95 percent mental, and the other half is physical." Yogi wasn't so good at math, but he sure as heck understood human nature and the competitive spirit when he made that mathematical blunder (an intentional one, I am sure). Fear of failure is much worse than the failure itself. Failure is actually a great teacher. Fear is simply a debilitation mechanism.

Yogi was also a great baseball player and is now a member of the Baseball Hall of Fame because of his accomplishments. Yogi hit about .300, which means that he got hits about 30 percent of the time. Wow! How many tests have you gotten a 30 on? Was it satisfying? What would have happened if Yogi had become depressed by his performance and given up because he hit only 30 percent of the time? He never would have made it into the Hall of Fame, notwithstanding his clever and inaccurate quips. One of my favorites was when he was playing a golf scramble with some buddies, and he said something like this: "If I were out here playing by myself, I would much rather hit my own ball." A clever master of the obvious, Yogi was also able to look foolish and laugh at himself while remaining passionately hungry for success. Ironic as it may seem to some, Yogi is truly an excellent role model for all of us. He didn't take himself too seriously outside of work and yet remained professionally focused all the way into the Hall of Fame.

Selling through Leadership

My personal perspective on selling is that it isn't really selling, but rather it's helping others become more successful. Doing that effectively requires leadership thinking and leadership activity. This chapter is dedicated to reviewing leadership principles that may be applied to the selling/helping process with a desired outcome of stimulating thoughtful examination of your current methodologies, expectations, and selling practices.

A TRUE LEADER...SERVES PEOPLE'S BEST INTERESTS

Serving the interests of other people—colleagues, partners, and clients—should be a top priority for you as a sales leader, regardless of title or job responsibility. There should be no question about that priority. The questions, however, become the following:

1. What are the best interests of those people?
2. Are they also your interests?

3. Are those interests their own desires?
4. Do those interests come from a book or an employee manual?
5. Are they simply those dictated by the goals of your company or their company?

I believe that the top priority could be all of these, or none of these.

The following discussion points are based primarily on my opinion, except for some scientific information about our brains and nervous systems. You may or may not agree with what I write. That's OK. I hope you will draw your own conclusions in a thoughtful manner and be inspired to take action toward optimal commercial leadership. There is no exact science to determining what another's best interests are. Like statistics, this practice is useful but not exact. Knowing what is best for others is not easy and can be filled with incorrect assumptions, inappropriate actions, and one- or two-way misunderstandings. So, if this so-called important component of leadership is prone to errors and inexact, what is its real value as service?

Think about a few variables that likely become part of this effort to do what is best for others. They are detailed in the pages that follow.

EMPATHY

Empathy, compassion, and sympathy are all used to reflect people's efforts to get to know others better. When working with clients you should always attempt to put yourself in their shoes to better understand their challenges. Remember that the people who work at XYZ Company are also human; they have the need to have others understand them, care about them, and help them be successful at what they do. At the same time, what they want is not always what they need. Remember, you are supposed to work in their best interests. You may have to dig up a measure of courage to tell them that what they are asking for is neither a best practice nor an ideal way of doing what needs to be accomplished—which leads directly to the topic of communication.

COMMUNICATION
According to many surveys, communication is the number-one success factor, so it must be really important to communicate effectively. How can I know and understand with compassion what a prospect's desires, goals, and aspirations are without engaging in effective two-way communication? You have two ears and one mouth. Shouldn't you then be listening more than talking?

There are a variety of factors that make effective communication, whether verbal or written, difficult. Because we communicate in various ways, it is important to understand the differences between them. But recognizing the differences is not enough; we must also accept them. If we don't communicate with open minds, we will "hear" what is being communicated via our own speaker systems. If someone is in stadium mode and you can only hear in concert-hall mode, you may be prone to misunderstanding that someone. The following six variations in communication styles illustrate some simple contrasts to be cognizant of while exchanging information (communicating) with others.

1. *Finish-Oriented*. This communicator wants to find the most direct path to the goal line. "Let's net this out and get to the final

destination as quickly and succinctly as possible." There is likely little room for eloquence in this communicator's monologue or dialogue.

2. *Lingering.* This communicator is more of a talker who enjoys conversation. "Let's talk awhile and relax a bit during conversations (including written ones)." The engagement itself is where the real value is to this individual.

Conclusion: These styles could prove difficult for one or both communicators, not strictly in their desire to get a point across or understand one, but emotionally as well.

3. *Emotional.* This communicator is more expressive during communication. Showing emotion is key to making a point or showing understanding. Such communicators simply are expressive of emotions during exchanges; it doesn't always mean that they are either upset or overjoyed.

4. *Strictly Factual.* These communicators want to stick to the facts and leave feelings and opinions out of the conversation—at least, so they think. The difficulty with this idealistic approach is that most people who claim to stick to the facts also provide bias and prejudice that color the conversation and the facts.

Conclusion: Have you ever tried selling while you are communicating very expressively, but you get a cold-hard-facts person to interact with? How did that feel?

5. *Trigger-Happy.* Such communicators can't wait to tell you what they are thinking, and they do a whole lot of thinking out

loud. They are likely not hearing, even when "listening," and so they will interrupt if in a verbal exchange or not fully consider what they are reading in a written exchange. Their "yes, but" style can break down effective communication in a hurry and confound other people very quickly. This doesn't necessarily indicate ill intent, but it can be a barrier to effectiveness.

6.   *Fair.* The communicator who waits her or his turn and doesn't jump in with both feet is being considerate and is likely attempting very intentionally to hear what is being said. Though there's no guarantee, it is more likely that people hear when they are not spewing thoughts aloud.

Conclusion: A fair communicator could appear to be dominated by one who is trigger-happy, but make no mistake: being intentional, thoughtful, and calculated can win the day.

Obviously, communication comes in a variety of forms and presents numerous challenges. Effectiveness of communication really depends on the situation and the other person's ability to understand what is being communicated. I'm not sure that my style preferences are correct; in fact, I am pretty certain that I may be completely wrong a significant amount of the time when making sales calls. Two ears and only one mouth, but as I said before, I think it is because true hearing is more important than speaking or even simply listening.

Be attentive to the words of my mouth.

—Proverbs 7:24

Following are some tips that may enhance your listening and hearing skills.

Listen with Your Face. Most relevant, literally, in the context of face-to-face interaction, this involves looking at the person who is speaking and focusing on what the person has to say.

Apply the same level of focus when reading written communication, and attempt to hear what people are saying through their written words. After all, you want them to focus on the important things that you have to say, don't you?

Hear. To me, hearing is the act of understanding what is being written or said, and it goes beyond reading or listening. Maintain a positive attitude, and choose to respond rather than react. Developing this skill requires taking a bit of time, some focus, and thoughtfulness. Let the other person's words sink in and analyze the information, and then you can better understand it.

Clarify. As you analyze information, ask clarifying questions and summarize to the other person what you think you hear. You are not only showing interest, but you are helping yourself to better understand what is being communicated. The same holds for written communication. There is nothing wrong with asking for clarification.

Filter. Focus more on what is being said than how it is being said. Body language, tone of voice, inflection, volume, and other characteristics of speaking can be deceiving. I know that body language and those other factors communicate something, but that something could simply be nervousness. Such factors can distort the speaker's real message if you allow them to influence you too strongly. Ben and Jerry's Coffee Toffee Bar Crunch tastes the same at the factory as it does at the store in downtown Manhattan.

The same holds true with regard to written communication. I often personalize my message in leadership writings to sound more like I am speaking. To some that may seem elementary, unprofessional, or even corny at times. But in every case, my intent remains the same—to communicate a message to help others be more successful.

Always filter style and delivery approach from the content.

After listening or reading beyond the style or delivery method so that you can better understand, you can then express yourself in a way that best facilitates effective two-way communication. Carefully chosen words are always the best method of expression. Following are some tips to help you find those words.

Think First. Speak or write only when you know what you really want to say or convey. The timing of your communication is also important. Being certain of what you want to communicate and when you want to do so takes some thought. Hopefully that thought will in turn provide clarity on how to be more effective.

Silence Is Sometimes Golden. Sometimes saying nothing is best. That is why it is often recommended that e-mail messages sit awhile in a drafts folder before transmission. I find that I will often make changes to an e-mail if I have delayed sending it. I had a friend who often would hesitate before responding to what he had just heard. I knew what he was doing; he was counting to ten. It gave him time to cool off, think about his response, and just plain respond versus react to what he had read. I have always admired, but I have not always been able to emulate, that behavior.

Have you ever heard the expression, "This silence is deafening"? Not saying anything can sometimes be the most effective approach. The truth is that some of what you are thinking sometimes remains better unsaid. A closed mouth gathers no feet!

Use Encouraging Words. Speaking with encouraging words is an art that requires a certain spirit and intentional effort. I suppose that one could make it a habit by repeating the effort enough. Whether it becomes second nature or not, trying to encourage others will likely be far more effective than continuously attempting to discourage them. If you work at maintaining the mind-set and heart-set of encouraging people in order to inspire and motivate them, I believe you will be much more effective communicators.

Establish Your Motivation. What you want to get from leading or managing people is a very important, distinguishing characteristic. As leaders who manage people, we all have "titles." Our titles, status, prestige, and paychecks are the "fame" that comes with our positions. However, leadership should be what you give, and that should be your first priority. So what is my motivation when considering the best interests of others? Should it be what I get from my position or what I give by providing help to others, with their success in mind? For years I have subscribed to the idea of always giving more than I take so that I never have to feel guilty. The motivation of leadership as service fits in with that idea, because the focus is on giving away all that I can to others for their benefit. Warren Bennis, author of *Learning to Lead: A Workbook on Becoming a Leader,* wrote, "Managers are people who do things right, and leaders are people who do the right thing." The right thing for servant leaders to do is to put others ahead of themselves.

I also believe that there are many people who are very good at the science of managing others in terms of making sure that procedures are followed, processes are completed, and spreadsheets are balanced. Unfortunately, I see far fewer people responsible for others who encourage, inspire, and motivate them to do great things. Those who encourage, inspire, and motivate are real leaders who turn good companies into great ones. These leaders need not have management titles; they simply have to want to be leaders and to keep developing themselves. When you are working in a sales role with prospects or clients, you need to adhere to the same principles if you really want to be a servant leader.

A TRUE LEADER... IS MOTIVATED BY LOVING CONCERN AND NOT PERSONAL GAIN

It is in our nature as humans to put ourselves first. None of us can honestly deny that. When you desire to become a true leader in the sense of servant leadership, you have to intentionally, consciously, and continuously work at overcoming that natural instinct to be number one. For me, the only way to overcome this powerful and innate obstacle is to intentionally, consciously, and continuously occupy your mind with thoughts that change the way your nature reacts to circumstances and situations. Then you must practice what you have taken in. You must repeat—repeatedly—the practices of effective leadership. You may not always do your best, but you must stay with it to improve. Becoming a better leader is not something you are born with. You may be born with a tendency toward a desire to lead (although I personally doubt that), but you can only become better at leading through continuous effort.

Our emotions come from our autonomic nervous systems; you don't control your emotions directly. You can try to contain them, hide them, and deny them, but however you determine to not allow your emotions to be sensed by others or affect your actions, you can't directly control the emotions themselves. When I get angry, I am angry. I can attempt to manage that anger, but I can't directly prevent it from occurring. When I get happy, I am happy in the same way.

The autonomic nervous system (ANS) is like a computer. The software loaded into the computer determines what it will do and how it will calculate input. If you load bad software (often referred to as "garbage") into a computer, you often get undesirable results that need to be corrected. The ANS is no different from the computer. If you are constantly feeding it with thoughts of self, self, self, and no one else, you will likely find it very difficult to be an effective servant leader.

A TRUE LEADER... IS MORE CONCERNED ABOUT THE PEOPLE THAN THE POSITION

If I place my fame (position or title) before the job I have to do as a leader, I will lose sight of what I really should be focusing on, which is the success of my team (others). If I focus on doing the job of helping others, the people in my company and our customers will succeed.

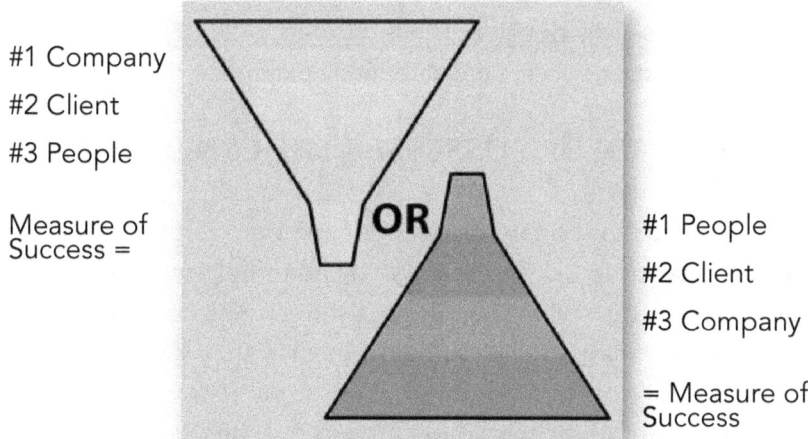

#1 Company

#2 Client

#3 People

Measure of
Success =

#1 People

#2 Client

#3 Company

= Measure of
Success

Figure 1 Reverse Philosophy Putting People First

I often use the image illustrated in Figure 1 of an upside down funnel (red) to illustrate contrasting leadership styles. In my methodology, the people I am responsible for in my company are at the top, clients are in the middle, and the company is at the bottom. The wide opening of that funnel is where I see opportunities for success. Nowhere on that funnel do the words "me" or "I" appear. The adage "There is no I in TEAM" may be old school, but then some things, like toothpaste and deodorant, seem to never go out of style either. Putting people first has made a significant difference, in my experience, and when the reverse occurs and the company is #1, success is limited, as illustrated by the narrowing opening at the bottom of the green funnel.

Ideally, focusing on people first will motivate them to do the same for others. They will care more because they are cared for. Caring for your internal teammates may inspire them to provide better service, ideas for success, and generally a stronger partner relationship. Your joint clients will, in turn, reward the company in the form of repeat business, good references, and expanding product ideas. This doesn't always happen, of course, but based on my own experiences, I can cite many examples of success.

A TRUE LEADER... POSSESSES THE CONFIDENCE TO SERVE

A major factor that prevents people from being good leaders is their reluctance to ask for help. We all need help to improve our performance, capabilities, and effectiveness. The problem is that some do not want to ask for help because they lack the confidence and/or courage to do so. They likely fear being viewed as incompetent or incapable of carrying out their responsibilities effectively. The truth is that those who do not ask for help are the ones who lack something and will be unable to serve others well in a leadership capacity.

In my own case, I simply lacked the confidence to ask. Until I gained that confidence, I also wanted to look good in the eyes of everyone around me and feel secure about my position. That security was false. I remember being at sales conferences and looking at other salespeople and thinking that they must have had something special that I didn't have. Eventually I learned that I was wrong. I was viewing the world through glasses that were not yet fear resistant. Mind you, I still have fear, but now I deal with my fear much differently. I am, essentially, comfortable being uncomfortable.

In order to genuinely be a sales leader, you have to be confident doing certain things. A few of those things are

- giving others credit instead of taking it yourself;
- trusting others to do their jobs effectively;
- allowing others to make mistakes when trying to do the right things;

- taking some arrows for the team in order to shelter them;
- accepting other ways of doing things; and
- putting others in the spotlight to allow them to shine.

Only when you become confident with who you are and how effectively you are leading will you be able to serve others, including your prospective clients, in a leadership capacity.

It is important that company leaders such as CEOs exhibit outstanding leadership qualities by having the confidence to seek advice and assistance. If the CEO can do that, I sure as heck can, too. What about you, Sales Professional?

There are many outstanding sales-training programs available on the market such as Miller Heiman, the EDGE, Lee Dubois, Franklin Covey, Sandler, and others. I have attended so many over the years that I don't even recall some of the program names. Each one possesses unique attributes that make it special, and each has specific methodologies that apply very much to the science of selling. The Lee Dubois method of selling was one of the early training courses that I took, and I remember it quite well. It was all about the art of selling (though systematic) and taught students to be extremely persistent and, in my opinion, pretty darned aggressive. I remember being taught to take twenty-one noes before giving up on a prospective sale. At the time I was following the formula to the letter, I was occasionally asked to leave establishments. Ironically, my boss at the time never had attended that sales training; consequently, we were not of the same school of thought. The EDGE contained some "art" as well, but it was also quite scientific. I found it to be effective and have incorporated some of its methods and principles in the concept of selling through leadership. However, I consider selling through leadership unique in that it is more of a philosophy than a methodology.

Brian A Mitchell

My thoughts or views stem from my own internal desire to lead; I thereon formulate methodologies or use sales skills to develop my particular operating style. Yogi might have described selling through leadership as 90 percent inspiration and 50 percent skill.

When leading a commercial team, I may include specific methodologies from previous training courses that I will ultimately tailor to best fit the needs of that team. For example, a specific CRM (customer relationship management) system is very useful tool for tracking leads, prospects, research, and tasks. For a CRM system to be used effectively, I believe it must be (1) easy to use, (2) simple to understand, and (3) standardized for everyone using, reviewing, or reporting from it. I have used several different systems over the years and have found the worst to be the most comprehensive and the best the simplest. I am a sales guy, not a financial analyst. I only need a few data elements to help me sell effectively. For me, CRM tools need to respond like a big, "flame throwing," left-handed pitcher with a ninety-seven-miles-per-hour fastball when advised, "Don't think too much, just rare back and fire that heater!" If a salesperson spends lots of time inputting data, analyzing data, and creating reports from a CRM system, he or she is not focusing as necessary on trying to help prospects, clients, and colleagues to be more successful.

When afforded the flexibility, I have tried to reconfigure systems to make them easy and standardized for all users. Then, when a CRM is not optimal, it can be changed—not a big deal. When not wed to some complex mechanism, change is easier. The KISS principle (Keep It Simple, Stupid!) continuously plays in my head like a beautiful melody. An entire team can learn to use a simple system in the same way, and then each teammate is able to cover for others when needed, handle others' calls, and often answer questions about situations within the others' frames of reference. All this can happen when information in the system is standardized for all users.

I also believe in evaluating the sales pipeline simply and in a standardized manner. If all have a few simple, descriptive sales-stages or deal-status categories, all will understand the entire pipeline to a reasonable extent. You the salesperson will have a better idea of where you are with each opportunity and be able to forecast accurately.

When sales stages and steps to close deals are simple, well defined, and clearly communicated, you will then be able to answer questions about the pipeline with accurate and supportable answers. Knowing what and who will be involved, that is, having specific dates and steps in place, will provide a guidance system to the close of the deal. Knowing the details of the deal, knowing the prospective client, and conducting planning activities as appropriate and necessary are very important.

Because communication is so important and the delivery of highly effective presentations is a crucial goal, a standard practice of mine is to establish an effective framework for what I call WOW (winning over winners) presenting. Some of what is used to establish the framework is based on past learning from various trainings, and some is original, based on the creativity and innovation of the sales team. I believe that each individual and each team have their own unique potential and that sales leaders can help shape tools, like presentation methodologies, to meet the market needs, product requirements for definition, and strengths of the sales team.

PASSION
Seeking the truth about someone's best interests will require unmasking her or him, and doing so takes significant effort on the

servant leader's part. But it is worth it; knowing people better will enable you to help them with what they need to achieve their best. If Chris, a sales rep who reports to me, has a specific desire to succeed, I should know that. If Chris has an unusual handicap that could be a hindrance under normal circumstances, it would be very helpful if I knew that, too. It would equip me to help him overcome the handicap and fulfill his potential to succeed.

Think of this also in the context of the existing client or prospect. You often hear "trusted adviser" used to describe how you want clients to perceive and treat you. I personally believe that many, if not most, people don't take that concept seriously enough, and they do not do what it takes to actually thrive in that role for their client companies. Seeking the truth in this case means getting to know the prospective client through and through and having the deep desire to help the client be successful. Master truth seeking, and the client will know and almost certainly respond in a positive manner. When your desire shows through, you will have earned the right to be considered a trusted adviser.

Selling through leadership is as much a way of thinking as it is a way of doing the sales job. In essence, this way of thinking leads to the doing. The focus is always on helping others to be successful and doing so with a mentality that reflects such leadership characteristics as good communication, courage in decision-making, continuous innovation, consistent passion, and a desire to serve with a vision for positive results. The how-to of the job falls into place like a well-rehearsed orchestra following its conductor!

Preparation

I once heard former New York City mayor Rudy Giuliani say that one can never be "too prepared." I had heard that before, but I questioned the sentiment; it's fine to be adequately prepared, I thought, but why spend more time preparing than is needed? Rudy's words sounded great, but they didn't fully resonate with me at the time. He said that he and his team were able to effectively respond to the 9/11 emergencies because they were "overprepared."

A year later, my initial view of what Mayor Giuliani had said that day changed forever. Personal experience often has that effect, doesn't it? I was asked to speak at the Burlington, Vermont, Elks Club annual memorial service. I felt honored to be asked to speak, so I accepted the invitation. When I met with the officials at the club, I found out that I was not only participating in their most significant event of the year, but that I was also the keynote speaker.

For years I strove to be adequately prepared, by arming myself with one and one-half to three times the preparation material that would actually be needed for the allotted time.

As the day approached when I would show up in front of 150–200 family members and friends of those Elks Club members who had died that year, I became more and more anxious and obsessed about my preparation and presentation. It got to the point where I couldn't decide precisely how to begin and end the twenty minutes I had to deliver the memorial talk. Normally, a pastor of a local church conducted the memorial service. I guess that all the local pastors were busy that year and that for some reason I was chosen to substitute. I was really out of my comfort zone with this event; I had never done anything close to what was required of this role. The families were likely still in some stage of mourning the deaths of their loved ones, and there I was, not familiar with any of them, to honor the deceased and provide comfort to the audience. Wow! Gulp! Thinking about it still puts a lump in my throat and brings tears to my eyes.

When the day came and I arrived at the service, I was blown away by the formality of the ceremony. I was very humbled and impressed with how the families' deceased loved ones were being honored. As I sat in the front row watching the activities, I became totally confused about what I would say or when I would say it. There were, it seemed, a thousand different thoughts and ideas darting around in my head.

When it was time for me to get up and speak, I just decided that whatever came out would come out. Thank God for being overprepared! I had much more topical material and supporting scripture prepared than I could possibly fit into a twenty-minute talk, and it paid off. Thank God also for moving my mouth and pushing out the words. I just went up to the podium and talked from my heart. It was really quite an amazing experience—one of the more surreal situations that I have ever participated in.

The talk went so well that multiple people approached me after the service and asked what church I preached at. I promptly thanked and humbly informed them that the talk had not been delivered by anyone qualified to be a preacher. Overpreparation rescued me that day; I will never again think of overpreparation as unnecessary.

I have often stated that in a selling situation, there is no such thing as being overprepared. Every bit of preparation can assist with handling the proverbial curve ball or changeup or with digging a little deeper to provide some added value during the meeting. Remember, getting to the truth is critical, and preparation is the only way to begin that process effectively when already in a selling situation. Even research meetings can become extremely challenging without some initial understanding of the prospective client's environment to help initiate an effective line of questioning. If you are not prepared, you are "winging" it, so you had better be a great pilot. Preparation is best accomplished by first establishing priorities.

PRIORITY MANAGEMENT

Life is full of decisions that you have to make regarding how you utilize your time and your resources. Prioritization of activities or goals so you complete those of highest priority first is important. How you prioritize will often determine your successes in business as well as your true enjoyment of life. When in the process of prioritization, I often think of the a song performed by the band Rascal Flatts with lyrics that includes the words, "When you have to choose, I hope you choose the one that means the most to you."

Those words to me are all about managing priorities and making decisions that are in keeping with your goals, mission, vision, and values. Hopefully the decisions regarding company goals will converge with personal goals to be beneficial for teammates, clients, you, and your family.

Each day provides new challenges and requires decisions about what to do and when to do it. Establishing priorities or determining what is most valuable of all that you have to do is like having a guidance system for the day. Without a reliable guidance system, you could end up driving around Phoenix, Arizona, for an extra hour when you really want to head to the Grand Canyon. Here again, I'm speaking from experience.

My days used to be taken up by priority numbers one, two, and three. My number-one priorities get top billing and attention. If I worked only on number-three priorities, I would likely be doing the easy things that returned the least "bang for the buck." If I got pulled away from my number one, it was like being dragged away from my number-one lady friend, which is very painful! My decision to write this handbook became my number-one priority during my free, alone time. Priorities numbered two and above don't normally even make it onto my goal sheet.

Establishing your own priorities is very important, because without them, you will be reacting to everyone else's priorities. It's likely that you know exactly what that is like. The end result of not having priorities can easily range from lack of direction to a state of full-blown chaos.

But sometimes we cannot avoid priorities that are established for us. It happens to me all the time. I have my day scheduled, and someone drops a project with a short timetable for completion into my lap. When that happens I have to reprioritize and then head to my calendar to tweak my schedule. You should expect those types of projects and priority shifts and simply incorporate them into your planning process as best you can.

TIME MANAGEMENT

During lectures, presentations, coaching sessions, and training sessions I talk considerably about continuous improvement. I also write about continuous improvement and how small gains create momentum and help achieve additional gains. This type of intentional lifestyle can become a habit that keeps us moving toward mastery or the ideal. I consider continuous improvement in the area of time management to be very important. There are many books written on the subject. I deliver talks on time management and cannot condense a two- to four-hour talk into a few written paragraphs.

That said, I hope some of the ideas I provide here will help you become more efficient and effective. Time management is really important for us salespeople. We always need to be in learning mode; that state of mind is a prerequisite for our being able to continuously sharpen our skills. So how do we find the time to sharpen our skills and do so with enthusiasm? All of us are pretty darned buried with everyday work. Think about that everyday work for a bit. Is it strategic and thoughtfully conducted, or is it reactionary and not 100 percent necessary? As you think about your day's work, ask yourself, "What will happen if I don't do this task?" Can you live without doing it and not suffer personally or professionally? Can you live without doing it and not make someone else suffer as a result? When it comes to making decisions about your everyday work and special projects, time management becomes critical.

If you don't manage your time, your time will manage you!

Without establishing priorities, time management is not possible. Without time management, productivity will suffer. After you establish your priorities, they have to fit into your daily schedule. In addition to your daily schedule, you have projects—hopefully mostly proposals—that you need to complete that will take an extended period of time. Those projects are more difficult to time manage. You have to break those projects into time chunks and incorporate those chunks into your daily schedule in order to meet your deadline. If you do that, you'll avoid stressing over your progress because everything will be scheduled out to completion, and you will see visible progress each step of the way. You also guard against procrastination, a great enemy of managing time.

Most people maintain a to-do list to manage their time. That is a start. As a simple example of time management, here is a list for one of my days several years ago:

Daily To-Do List

Priority   Task Completed: x
1   Call SLU to get IDRR contract signed. x
2   Call John at UIA to discuss storage architecture.
3   File expense report.
1   Call ISC regarding IHC. x
2   Read Performance Review training document.
1   Review RSL agreement in for mtg. x
3   Review SDH storage architecture doc
3   Complete benefit enrollment.
1   Prep intro and close for webinar. x
1   Send invite to TH webinar to all customer lists. x

Projects

Priority	Task	Completed: x
1	Complete Introduction topic in Selling through Leadership handbook.	x
2	Develop webinar material, and practice presentation.	
3	Complete one training module.	
2	Do performance assessments.	
2	Develop upgrade campaign.	

Back then, there were days when I felt I did well with time management and other days when I felt like a complete flop. Have you ever experienced such ups and downs yourself? The particular day illustrated above went pretty well, considering I was on the phone in meetings for more than five hours. Otherwise, I would not have called it a good day.

Look at my list: There are ten to-dos and five projects staring me in the face. Only priority-one tasks were completed. And I didn't even include the five hours of phone meetings. I get tired just thinking about it. I put forth plenty of effort, but where were my results?

Below is a more recent daily plan for me, where you will notice a significant difference. I have evolved into realizing that I can no longer (nor ever could) "boil the ocean." Boiling the ocean became a favorite expression of mine a few years ago; it reminded my team and me not to overcommit but to try instead to really work smarter by managing our time and lives. Boiling the ocean, as the phrase implies, is simply trying to accomplish that which is beyond one's capabilities. Overcommitting either to ourselves or to others is not a healthy activity. Missing commitments can turn allies into enemies, prospective wins into losses, happy clients into dissatisfied clients, and confidence into insecurity and fear.

I no longer maintain a to-do list. I now thoughtfully manage a daily goals list that contains no more than five priority-A goals on it. That's right—only five. The list ties in directly with my weekly goals, which tie into my plan. Plans and goals do change, but a thoughtfully constructed list that reflects them at any given moment provides a really solid foundation for time management. Without them, all you'll have is a "to-do" list that will cause you to run around like a hen being chased by a hungry fox.

Daily Goals (Five A Priorities)

1. Return redlined agreement to XYZ with comments.
2. Follow up XYZ comments with a call to John Doe for discussion.
3. Call CEO of ABC Company to make an appointment to discuss my commercial plan to win proposal (this could take multiple attempts).
4. Return e-mails and phone calls.
5. Draft Selling through Leadership chapter of sales-training handbook.

There is room in this goal list for the unexpected. I also maintain a list of projects or actions to review and select from to develop my "A" list each day (actually most often the night before), but there is a huge difference between managing my time this way versus even a pretty efficient former way. What I learned was that completing a daily goals plan successfully has its rewards in the sense of satisfaction for accomplishing those goals. I am also managing my own expectations more realistically so as not to overcommit, even to myself. I continuously improve and win in step-by-step fashion; I no longer attempt to boil the ocean. Smaller winning days are still winning days, but always falling short can become discouraging and has no place in a continuous-improvement effort. It can build its own momentum. Winning builds confidence and positive momentum. Positive momentum is a very powerful force. It also helps us to better manage the expectations of others more effectively, and that alone, my friends, will dramatically reduce your stress levels.

It bears repeating: Manage your time, or it will manage you!

DEAL MANAGEMENT

When you do a good job of managing your time, you are also better able to manage your deals. Deal management is all about timing and thoroughness. If you want to be in control of a deal, you must understand the deal and the prospect's business, set action plans, and make commitments that you can deliver on. Then you must be rigorous about delivering what you promise.

With so many deals in the pipeline at the same time, we salespeople have to be excellent time managers. We also must be able to determine which deals are most important and require immediate attention. That can be a difficult task, given that most clients feel that they are number one or have urgent issues almost all of the time. Does this scenario seem familiar to you? Of course it does. It's your world. It's my world, too. So the question becomes, how do you determine which deal is most important and requires immediate attention?

The most common management technique is the old "squeaky wheel gets the grease" method. But that method of deal management is reactive and will rarely, if ever, allow you to be in control. When you operate that way, you are the dog being wagged by the tail. Saying that you will never operate that way again is really stretching it, but surely it does not have to be the rule. Make it the exception, and see how much better control you have, how much clearer you think, how much more productive you are, and how much more sane you become.

How do you avoid being controlled by the customer or colleague? You do so by having the courage and conviction to manage expectations properly. If you never tell people that you can't get something done by 3:00 p.m. today, but you really can't get it done, what happens? You either ignore them and do what is on your priority list, or dump all of your other number-one priorities and jump on the 3:00 p.m. deadline task.

What are the consequences of such behavior? In the first option, you will upset the person requesting the 3:00 p.m. deadline by ignoring the request. In the other scenario, you will upset several other people, including yourself, by missing multiple commitments when you drop them for this 3:00 p.m. project. You lose in both situations. Is there an alternative? Of course there is an alternative. All it takes is a little thought and some guts. Think about what realistically can be accomplished and when it can be completed, and then have the guts to deliver that message with conviction. The courage part may be the most difficult, but the thought part will ultimately determine your long-term success.

Setting expectations and adjusting commitments can be very unpopular. But if you consistently deliver when you say you will, it will be easier over time for you to (1) reset expectations effectively and (2) gain acceptance of adjustments. Trust is typically built over time. Distrust is frequently developed in an instant. Overcommit, and watch what happens. A pattern of early demands will likely follow because you will not be considered dependable.

LIFE MANAGEMENT

Managing our time and priorities and setting expectations are not just activities for working hours. Management of our lives in general is critical to our contentment and often our health. For workaholics like me, balancing life and work is a formidable task that never ceases to challenge. I find myself working seven days a week more often than not. And why shouldn't I? I grew up milking cows seven days a week, fifty-two weeks a year. It's in my DNA. Don't get me wrong: I love leisure time. As I get older, I find leisure to be more and more pleasant. Yet I still find myself working Saturday and Sunday nearly every weekend.

So is there any hope for me? I think so, because I also try to balance the work with time away from work. I cherish time with my beautiful wife. I love the invigoration of pounding my way through trees or bumps in deep snow at twelve thousand feet above sea level in the Rockies. And perhaps more than anything, I crave camping in the great outdoors and hiking for hours at a time, where I think of nothing more than what wild animal I might see as I round the next bend in the trail.

In addition my spiritual life is critical to my contentment. With sometimes intense stress at work, my resting place is within my spiritual being. I am not always the person I want to be, and when I need to get regrounded and refreshed, I know where to go. Without my study and prayer life, I would be in a downward spiral that gets caught in the winds of the world and tossed about like the waves on Lake Michigan on a nasty day. I take spiritual breaks during tough days. They may last for only ten minutes and come between conference calls or meetings, but those little walks make a huge difference in my life's balance. I also find that beginning my day with prayer and study gets it started the right way.

You may have a different way to maintain balance in your life. It may be hunting, fishing, shopping, riding a motorcycle, researching wine, running, getting your nails done, or throwing darts. Whatever it is, work cannot be the be-all and end-all for you, or you will be swallowed up in its insatiable appetite for mind and body. If you become fully consumed by work, your personal life will suffer greatly; that is simply not healthy and not worth the cost.

Making time to do what you love outside of work is important to your success in life and your success at work. Being refreshed will help you be more productive and energized. Both of these states are critical if you are to reach your unique potential. Both of these states are essential for you to achieve greatness.

Persistence

You have probably heard the old saying, "Nothing worth having will come easily," and the shorter statement, "Persistence pays." To me these statements mean (1) achieving what I want when I want it may take some additional or even extraordinary effort, and (2) if I keep at something long enough and with determination, I just may be able to achieve it, even when it is difficult.

Persistence means continuing to put forth a focused effort to attain a goal. Abraham Lincoln's journey to become who many consider to be one of the greatest presidents of the United States illustrates an incredible example of persistence.

Lincoln's Road to the White House

- Failed in business in 1831
- Defeated for legislature in 1832
- Second failure in business in 1833
- Suffered a nervous breakdown in 1836
- Defeated for speaker in 1838
- Defeated for elector in 1840
- Defeated for Congress in 1848

- Defeated for Senate in 1855
- Defeated for vice president in 1856
- Defeated for Senate in 1858
- Elected president in 1860

Being persistent requires courage. Fear, an emotion we know all too well, often blocks us from exhibiting courage. Reconsider a process, albeit oversimplified, that was described earlier in this book: Emotions emanate from our autonomic nervous system (ANS) and largely cannot be controlled. But if we feed good information into our brains, then more useful emotions will be more likely to assume more control in our psyches.

How do you effectively renew your mind to reduce fear of failure, which you must somehow overcome to be persistent? The simple answer is to build confidence through positive input into your mind. It doesn't mean you won't fail, but it does mean you are confronting your fear. I believe that if you continually confront your fears, you will become more comfortable doing so. Become more comfortable with confronting your fears, and you create a "new normal" way of living and proceeding.

It is courageous to be able to accept failure as part of success. By using failure as the great teacher that it is, you learn and grow. Lincoln withstood significant failures to learn how to succeed in being elected president. If you are a reflective type of person, now may be a good time to reflect on your failures and determine what you have learned from them.

Good sales leaders will wisely and lovingly foster a culture that encourages risk taking without being afraid to fail. When people can take risks without fear of retribution, they become more confident, innovative, and creative—and they close more sales.

As one who has failed many times, I am blessed with the desire to allow people to fail in order to improve. It wasn't something that I thought about and then instituted; instead, it stemmed from a heart-centered desire to help others become successful, content, happy, and motivated in their work. I have experienced a lot of fear and have had to develop an intentional behavioral process of stepping out of comfort and into fear to grow. Therefore, I have great empathy for others who dare to be different to get better at what they do and become more content with their lives.

FINDING OPPORTUNITIES

Finding opportunities is sometimes quite easy and other times really difficult. Sometimes economic conditions affect the availability of opportunities. Other times, your existing client base can have an effect on how easily you can find new opportunities. The many other variables that can have an impact on the process include

- brand recognition;
- industry reputation;
- competitive landscape;
- legislative impact;
- business longevity;
- your personal experience in the industry;
- your product knowledge; and
- your willingness to step out of your comfort zone.

Some of these variables are out of your control and have to be dealt with in specific and strategic ways. Others are within your control and must be dealt with head on if you wish to go from good to great as a salesperson or commercial professional.

Prospecting for opportunities can be difficult for some be-cause you don't know where to begin and/or you despise cold-calling. If you are one of those people, join the club. When I was a rookie salesman with the Burroughs Corporation in Burlington, Vermont, we were trained to cold-call prospects and to not leave an account before taking twenty-one noes. At the time we were tasked with selling oversized, underfunctioning, and overpriced calculators. We were given what was called a "green sheet" to track our calls each day and directed to make as many cold calls as we could. You can imagine what it was like some days when I was traveling the back roads of Vermont with the calculator and my instructions about taking noes. I was actually told to leave on more than one occasion; I was more politely asked to leave on many other occasions. I did learn a great deal from that experi-ence, but I don't really subscribe to that formula for professional development today.

In fact, there is absolutely no reason to make a completely cold call. Anyone who is cold-calling a customer is simply lazy and not following intelligent or proper procedure. With a bit of rigor, you can almost always find something to talk about with the client when you call. If nothing else, the Internet is a very good source of information that can take some of the chill out of the cold call. I will channel Professor Roberts and proclaim, "This is key. Never cold-call a prospect!" Besides the Internet, most of us have a network of people who could help break the ice of a call. It may not always happen, but it is often possible to find people who will make some sort of introduction for you. But you must be willing to take the time, exhibit the courage, and make the effort to ask around a bit.

Not only do you often have former colleagues and clients who would help, but you may also have people in your own company or a partner organization who would help make an introduction. If you can't find any of those folks, how about getting in touch with college or high school friends, family friends, or friends of friends of friends? Get the picture?

> *Individual commitment to a group effort—that*
> *is what makes teams work, a company work, a*
> *society work, a civilization work.*
>
> —Vince Lombardi

Remember, TEAM stands for "Together Everyone Achieves More."

UNDERSTANDING THE DEAL

The more you know about the customer, the deal that you are working on, or what to prospect for, the more ammunition you have for winning. When we used the EDGE sales process at GE Healthcare, we were provided with two excellent tools to either reference, if already completed, or build in order to gather valuable intelligence.

1. BUSINESS UNDERSTANDING DOCUMENT

The business understanding document (BUD) can be very helpful for storing all the intelligence gathered about a particular customer. Knowing the decision-makers, the influencers, the gate-keepers, the coaches, and the dissenters in an organization is very helpful when prospecting or trying to close a business deal. You can enter all the information in a CRM system as well in a separate, formatted document. The point is that a BUD of some sort, because intelligence is built into it, is a very valuable tool. As previously mentioned, there are all sorts of places to gain a business understanding of a new prospect. The Internet, the news, other clients, friends, and current and former colleagues are all good sources of intelligence to build a BUD.

2. OPPORTUNITY PLANNER

The opportunity planner (OP) was the other EDGE document that we used at GE Healthcare. The OP focuses in a more laser-like manner on a specific opportunity than on a client's business in its entirety. As with the BUD, the OP can be part of a CRM system for a simpler and easier approach to documenting an opportunity. At the very least, any documents used for opportunity planning should be attached to the opportunity in a CRM system.

By having an OP at your fingertips, you can quickly get a summary of what the keys to the deal are, a realistic look at the opportunity, the needed next steps, the current positioning, and who the key players are. Once again, some rigor is required to develop and maintain the OP, but it is a great habit to develop and does not require much work. Simply document the objectives of the prospect initiative, the key decision-makers, the budget and/or funding process, and the steps to get to close, with dates, individuals, and work required to get there. The OP is yet another form of road map that can lead to closing the deal.

Regardless of the tool used, research, asking questions, and a relentless effort to get to the truth is imperative for optimizing the process and achieving the highest level of success for both client prospect and your business. It is all part of creating a win-win arrangement.

Professionalism

Professionalism simply equates to doing the right things at the right time during the sales cycle. I don't think that's an oversimplification. Selling is much like soccer to me; they are both really simple games that some will attempt to make complex because they don't break the two activities down to their basics and view them that way. In some instances people do that because they don't understand those basics. In both activities, understanding the processes is critical. By having a full understanding, executing the fundamentals methodically will generate wins.

Here's an example of both the sport of soccer and the profession of selling. If I am teaching ball-striking in soccer practice, I will break down the execution to foot positioning when approaching the ball, body balance, eye contact, the execution of the strike, and the follow-through motion to complete the pass or shot. It's very simple really, yet some get so wound around the axle trying to teach it that they confuse their students, and execution never becomes what it should be.

Professionalism in selling is similar. If you follow the basic steps outlined in this handbook, selling is quite simple, isn't it?

It is when you attempt to do things out of the ordinary, perform tasks out of order, or skip steps altogether that you add complexity to the process. There are no real shortcuts, and if you try to eliminate steps, you are almost certain to have to return to those steps later. And you will likely have to do so in more adverse conditions because you didn't include them in the first place. For example, if you go to step eight in the sales process and skip everything else, you will almost certainly have to backtrack. When backtracking, you will probably find out that your forecast is inaccurate. Ouch! In addition, you may discover some technical or business gotchas that you weren't aware of, and suddenly your credibility is at risk, and your deal is in jeopardy.

I remember an advertisement for Fram oil filters, whose message was "pay me now, or pay me later." I will never forget it, because it rings so true for many of our investments in time, products, or personal development. It also holds true for investment in efforts to close a sales deal. You need to follow the process and be professional about it, or you will quite often face issues later on that can be costly. There are no shortcuts.

STAY ON TOP OF DEALS

Staying on top of deals is a classic example of professionalism in sales. To know the deal, you must stay on top of the deal. You keep your CRM and any other planning mechanisms current. You know where in the process your customers are so that you are in lockstep with their needs and timetables and so that you can add value to opportunities by really helping them meet their goals and overcome their challenges. To me, staying on top of a deal means being totally immersed in the deal from prospecting, through product delivery, to ensuring that the product is functioning properly. That, of course, requires diligence, rigor, courage, and continuous communication with the prospect and the entire team involved in the process.

MANAGE THE SALES CYCLE

Moving the deal along is important to meet the goals of both the prospect and your team. Why do you need to move the deal to help the prospect? The answer is often very simply that clients have goals and timelines established when buying products. The goals may range from deadlines for spending budgeted money to implementation scheduling to moving services to outsourcing or to upgrading technology in order to take advantage of other critical technology.

Whatever the reasons, you need to understand them and match up your goals, capabilities, and expectations with those of the prospect so that you can truly help the prospect and make her or his buying experience as easy and timely as possible.

Again, it is important to understand and follow processes so as not to leave out any information, skip any questions, or ignore any contracts or other requirements. When trying to stay in lock-step with customer expectations, capabilities, and timetables, you can't miss steps, or you will misstep. You must get documents, people, and procedures on both sides in synchronization to make sure that everything will be completed at the agreed-upon time.

FIND WAYS TO HELP OR PROVIDE VALUE

Finding new ways to provide success to clients is a mantra that you should always do your best to live by. After all, if you are not in this business to help clients be successful, you should not be in this business. There are few things more satisfying to me than experiencing the success that a client realizes because I helped them. Wow! I get a rush every time that I think about that.

There are so many ways that you can help your clients and add value to their buying experience. It can happen before, during, or after they actually buy something, or it may be as a direct result of them purchasing from you. A former GE Healthcare colleague, Jerry Lynn, and I once worked on a technical infrastructure opportunity for Springfield Service Corporation (SSC), where we followed up the work done with a promotional video. Through some work with our partner, HP, we were able to get the video funded so that all three companies involved would benefit, but HP would pay. I always really liked that part! The promotion featured the CEO of SSC, the director of IT, and me. The customer was delighted to tie its strategic partnership with HP and GE into a very powerful video sales tool. Of course, HP and GE were able to do the same, and all parties won as a result of that deal. That is just one example of adding value to a prospect or client.

In another good example, while still at GE Healthcare I worked with Intersystems Corporation (a database provider) on two large deals where both clients were ready to buy licenses that they didn't yet need. They were interested in those licenses because of anticipated growth, at a time of uncertainty regarding budget approval. They didn't want to be caught in a budget crunch and find users being locked out of their system due to the lack of licenses. What we were able to do allowed the client to grow as much as needed without expanding their licenses until the following fiscal year. Analysis of actual usage during the growth spurt provided a business case for budget justification to pay for the already in-use licenses. Both of those clients were absolutely ecstatic.

For several years now, I have been a strong promoter of a book titled *You Don't Need a Title to Be a Leader*, written by

Mark Sanborn. This book about leadership emphasizes doing little things to make a big difference. It was based on a true story of the behavior of perhaps the most famous mail carrier in the United States, Fred from Denver, Colorado. Fred very quietly became famous after people noticed all the little things that he did that had made an impact with his customers. Fred would take newspapers from the driveway and place them behind obstacles on the porch so as not to reveal that the homeowners were away. He did that to protect his customers from potential burglary or vandalism. Fred did enough of those types of little things to eventually be sought after by the media and authors. He has been honored on television, radio, in print, and by the US Postal Service.

As far as I know, Fred continued throughout his career as a mail carrier, not a manager. His story illustrates two things to bear in mind when dealing with your clients and prospects: (1) you don't have to have a manager's job to be a leader, and (2) the little things can make a big difference. Little things are those that are both easy to do and easy not to do. Your success rate can sometimes be a direct result of whether you do or don't do the little things for your clients.

Of course, there are many other ways that you can add value for your clients. You can periodically provide them with valuable information that will assist them with the work of improving their environments. You can also bring in your partners to provide more in-depth education about products, trends, and road maps for them. The more you can help them, the closer relationship you will have, the more invested you will become in their success, and the more gratifying your work with them will become.

I challenge you to try to find small and large ways to make a difference for your clients. Almost certainly, your rewards will be far greater than your efforts.

NEGOTIATE FOR A WIN-WIN

When you think about negotiating with a prospect, how do you feel? Does the thought make you uneasy? Does it make you fearful? Do you view negotiating as an art, a science, or a passion? I advise against getting too crafty when negotiating; craftiness can introduce deception into the process. I despise the old cloak-and-dagger method of negotiation, which implies subterfuge activity. After all, the word "negotiation" connotes give-and-take. So how should you approach negotiating?

You are already familiar with the colloquialism "win-win." It is used to describe a situation where both sides win, but it has no quantitative component. That is, it doesn't answer the question of who wins more. Now that's a great question, isn't it?

Back up a few sentences, and attempt to answer the questions posed there. Here they are again:

1. Does negotiating make you uneasy?
   If you say yes, I believe that you are in the majority. But is that where you want to be? Answer that question, too.
2. Does it make you fearful?
   Now I am getting personal, aren't I? Yes, I am, and I fully intended to. Let me be clear—there is absolutely nothing wrong with being fearful. How you deal with your fear is the real issue.
3. Do you view negotiating as
   a. an art?
   b. a science?
   c. a passion?

Write your answers down. You may want to refer back to them later.

Now consider the give-and-take concept. It implies that to give, you must take, and to take, you must give. Furthermore, if you take, you must give, and if the other party wants to take, it also must give. So far I like this stream of thought; it makes me feel balanced, fair, and helpful versus selfish and uncaring. How do you feel?

Here is some additional insight on the give-and-take and win-win concepts. Many books and other types of commentary address negotiating. Some of them approach it as an art; other approaches consider it scientific. I contend that negotiating consists of all three components shown above: art, science, and passion. Wanting desperately to provide a fair deal for your clients is a passion that will surely be noticed and likely is contagious.

In *Strategic Negotiation*, written by Brian Dietmeyer with Rob Kaplan, a great deal of science is applied to negotiating. A concept called consequences of no action (CNA) is detailed. Defining both seller and buyer, CNA requires a bit of artistry on both sides; some of the qualitative or even quantitative value of the "other" side's CNA is determined through deductive reasoning, inference, or simple gut feeling or intuition, in some cases. Estimating CNA is best accomplished by knowing as much about the truth of a given situation as possible. Questions such as the following must be answered:

- Will the prospect be able to implement the project timeline if negotiations break down and they have to begin anew with their second choice?
- Does the higher level of experience that your company brings to the table provide enough security for the

prospect to warrant them giving in to reduce liability on your part in this contract?

- Will the prospect be willing to pay more for your product because you have a local office versus going with their number-two choice that is not local?

At the end of the day, some clearly visible consequences that your prospect will want to avoid could emerge. Those are important to know if at all possible. There may also be consequences that you wish to avoid as well. If the business fit between two parties is outstanding, and the deal is critical to the growth goals of your company, then you may be willing to give up more to win than to hold tight to negotiating and lose to the competition.

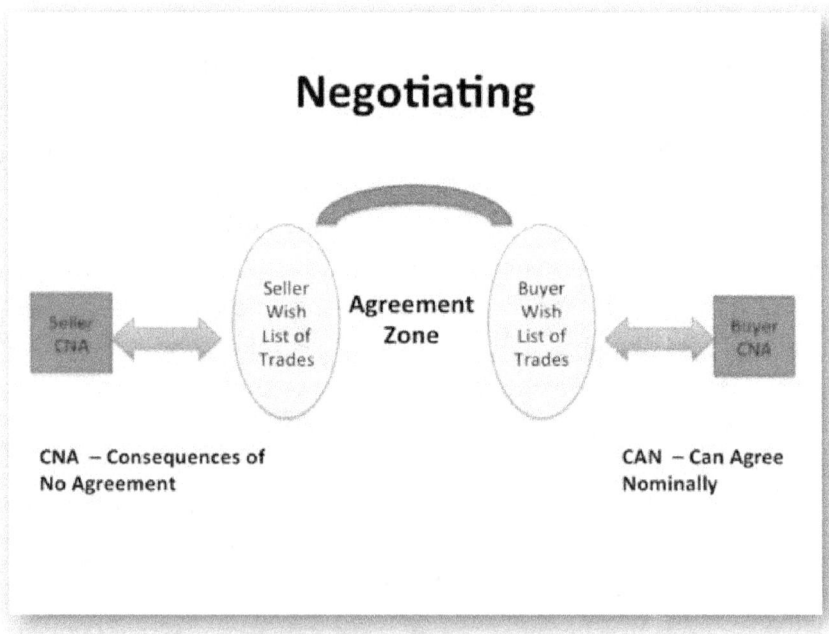

Strategic Negotiating 1

Another important concept explored is that of the negotiation wish list (Strategic Negotiating 1), which details what buyer and seller wish to gain and, conversely, are willing to give up to achieve desired results. Unless the other party is completely transparent, you need something more than science in order to calculate every wish list variable. So once again, knowing the truth is very important. Perhaps the one who fronts the negotiation for the prospect will want something and express it enthusiastically when the ultimate decision-maker does not apply the same priority to that wish-list item. How would you know unless you probed for the truth? Realistically, you may never go into negotiations armed with all of the knowledge you could use, but knowing as much as you can and then continuing to learn throughout the process are very important.

The goal in negotiating is to arrive at the agreement zone as illustrated. Some give-and-take may be required prior to arriving there. In addition to wish-list development, understanding the consequences of no agreement (CAN) is important. If you can't agree, you lose the sale and the revenue from that sale. What does the buyer lose if you can't agree? They will likely have to start the process over and then negotiate with someone else. And what if your product included a key differentiator that provided them with a competitive advantage or a compliance requirement? You will lose the sale, but they may have more serious consequences. In those situations, it may be profitable for both to agree nominally so that both parties win, even if not an ideal arrangement.

Adding value to the negotiation process is critically important. Wanting to help the prospect be successful is fundamental to bringing your best to the table during negotiations. There will be some situations where negotiating with the prospect doesn't ever really occur, but those situations are rare. During those times, the prospect may communicate that the best and final offer has to be made up front. Even then, there may be additional negotiations occurring after vendor selection is made. So a bit of wisdom would be to develop both sides of the wish list and keep some additional wishes in your back pocket just in case they are needed during final negotiations.

I wrote earlier of my dislike for cloak-and-dagger style negotiation. It reminds me way too much of the experience of buying a car when I was in my twenties and the incredible disingenuity of the salespeople at the dealerships. I still remember the feeling of having to be totally on guard and not trusting anything that they told me.

That said, I have two real-world examples of why having at least one more wish-list item—the one in my back pocket—provided a win-win situation for both the prospect and me. The first was an existing customer (as "clients" were known at the time) with whom I was completely transparent because I trusted him. Well, I found out that he was clever, shall we say, about negotiating with me. Apparently, his purchasing team sent me his approved requisition by mistake. Can you guess what I learned from that mistake? I learned that he was approved to spend more than he told me he was approved for. So what did I do the next time we were negotiating a deal for some product? I kept a little additional discount in my back pocket, so that when he asked for more discount, I had it to give. He was very happy with our deal. That was a win-win that required just a bit of wish-list enhancement on my part.

The second situation became a fun ritual for both the purchaser and me. She would always call me on the phone and address me as "Honey." I am laughing as I write this, because I always knew what was coming next: She always needed my help. And guess what? I was delighted to provide her with some additional help in the form of a small extra discount. Of course, knowing what was going to occur enabled me to properly prepare the win-win negotiation in advance of the actual conversation. I really love win-win transactions!

Building negotiating skills requires more than academic learning. Over time, experiential learning combined with the incorporation of proven or innovative ideas will help you become a special negotiator who has the ability to create win-win transactions. But one last required aspect of negotiation, beyond the building of the wish list, adding value, and the estimating the can, is the passion that you show for the making of a great deal. Selling through leadership is infused with passion for helping others be successful and knowing that a given result is the right thing for all concerned. Does it mean that saying yes to everything and giving away huge discounts and other valuable, costly assets is the only way? Absolutely not; in fact, that approach will almost certainly create a problematic deal that will at some point not be a good business fit. Finding value for both parties in what Dietmeyer (with Kaplan) refer to as the "agreement zone" is the best way to negotiate a transaction. That is where trades can be made that add value for one side without depleting value below the desired level for the other side.

KEEP YOUR WORD

This one is simple—do what you say you will. That's right; that's it. But is it as easy as it sounds? Hold on. Before you react, think about it. Is it really that easy to always do what you say you will? I think not, and I will give you one example of a time I made a promise that I did not keep—and regrettably I have made many over the years.

A few years ago my wife and I were inspired to look into adopting a child from the foster system in Colorado. We attended classes, met with experts, prayed, talked to others, attended group meetings, and did a significant amount of reading to prepare us to make the final decision and move ahead. I ultimately told an eleven-year-old that she was "home now" and that she would "never have to worry about having to move to another family again." I meant what I said; we were committed to providing the child a permanent family and a new normal in her life. Well, the Mitchell house soon became a house of terror, and I began to think of this youngster (affectionately of course) as our "little terrorist." I fell in love with the child but after an eight-month stretch of one "unnatural" disaster after another, through weeping eyes and a sobbing voice I had to inform her that she could no longer live with us. It still breaks my heart whenever I think about it.

I/we should have been more careful about our commitment to the child and more thoughtful and patient prior to making the commitment. We were just so darned excited about rescuing this poor little orphan from the misery of her past and giving her a new life that we zealously zoomed forward into the unknown, only to find that this pair of working parents without other children at home were not effectively equipped to meet her extensive needs. The bottom line is that I didn't keep my word.

So what can you learn from Brian Mitchell's *major* broken promise? I will share with you five things that I learned:

1. GUARD YOUR HEART
Decisions are sometimes made based on feelings without carefully thinking them through. Understanding what will be required to carry out a particular responsibility should always be considering before acceptance of that responsibility. Guarding your heart can be a concept applied to many different circumstances, but in the context of keeping your word, being careful to integrate your thinking with your feelings is wise. Doing so will mix some common sense in with the feelings surrounding the situation to provide balance and hopefully a more informed perspective and a more logical conclusion regarding commitments made.

2. DON'T MAKE DECISIONS WHEN YOU ARE EMOTIONALLY HEATED
Have you ever been upset with a fellow employee? How did you react? Did you do what I have done in the past: react with a violent temper, yell and scream, make a scene, threaten the person, and/ or talk behind his or her back? Of course you haven't, right? Many times when we react that way we create a much larger problem or challenge than we had in the first place. We may not think so immediately because we may have just won a little battle. What we likely didn't realize is that the war had just begun. Everything changed at that moment in time; we acquired a situation that we would then have to deal with for a much more extended period— perhaps many years. The stone that we had thrown into the pond

made a small splash, but soon everyone around us joined the action and starting throwing stones of their own. Somehow we had no idea that a ripple effect would occur throughout the organization and create a lasting wave of negativity. The takeaway here is that different handling of a situation would prevent any stones from being cast.

It severely dents my sensitive ego to recall my own heated situations. I realize that I should have walked away, counted to ten, or thought about lying on my favorite beach on a warm sunny day—something to avoid that tipping point. I could have returned later with a level head and tried to sort out my perceived challenge without causing my own war.

3. WAIT ON YOUR FINAL ANSWER FOR SOME TIME BEFORE MAKING IT KNOWN

The best way to put your own feet to the fire is to broadcast your intentions. I have talked many times to people about the idea of publicizing their New Year's resolutions. Are you laughing out loud and yet cringing at the same time? I have been there and done that and am almost certain that I am in a crowded room. So, how did you feel when you didn't stop eating ice cream or didn't drink only on weekends or went to the gym maybe once every other week versus four times a week or made a to-do list that included commitments to fellow employees and clients when there was no way in a very hot place that you could deliver? (Remember, that is why I develop a maximum of five "A" priority goals each day). Consider "sitting" on some decisions for a few days before announcing them. I know it is hard, but it is also rewarding in the event that I decide on a different direction during those few days. Did you ever change your mind about something? "Slow down and grill," as Kingsford Charcoal advises us. Think about things for a while, and then announce your decision.

4. BE MORE PATIENT

Corporate America today is generally very impatient. Public companies and venture-capital companies are even more impatient. And let's face it; we are becoming wired for instant gratification as the pace of life seemingly increases by the minute. I have often talked about the weekends flying by. Yes, they do—faster and faster and faster. Are we really so smart that we can make hasty decisions to keep pace with the acceleration around us and still develop sound, well-thought-out conclusions? Remember, we never dispose of any information taken into our brains. Also remember that our recall is not always instantaneous. I would bet that we all hate waste of any kind and likely try to minimize the amount we waste. So why waste decisions by being hasty? Or put another way, why waste valuable time by not using it to make sound decisions? Head back to the patio, and grill those thoughts a bit longer so that they become "well done."

5. BE AT PEACE WITH YOUR DECISIONS

Once again I can provide an illustration from my own experience of the incredible importance of being at peace with decisions.

When I left an employer after sixteen years of success, I went to a start-up company with great promise—right time, right market, right product, and, I thought at the time, the right approach. A few months later, I found myself frustrated by and regretful of my decision to make this change. I did not regret leaving the sixteen-year job, because that was a great although difficult decision; I regretted my current situation. Yuck! So one day, after much thought, prayer, and consultation with my wife, I decided to become unemployed for the first time in nearly twenty-five years.

I decided to resign from that start-up company. How would I explain myself to the company? What would it feel like to tell friends and family about my decision? How would it affect my financial situation (I had always been the largest breadwinner in my family)? Well, I am here to tell you that my only regret is that I didn't quit before I started that job. Instead, I let my pride get in the way of my decision-making. OK, let me emphasize that: my *pride* got in the way! Sometimes it takes extra measures of courage to really look inside and around us to come to the right conclusions. I, a Type A, seven-days-a-week, former farm boy, took my time, gathered all the courage I could muster, and, after resigning, could honestly say, "What a feeling of relief!"

What was my secret? There was none! To reiterate, I stepped back, took my time, had some courage to look inside, and then forcefully moved my pride aside. As a result, I had as much clarity as I ever had had before, and I knew that I had made a decision that was right for my family and me.

Meeting commitments to clients, partners, or coworkers is critical to developing integrity, trust, and credibility. Essentially, when you say you are going to do something, you need to make certain you do it. If for some unforeseen reason you have to change that commitment, you must immediately communicate that and develop an alternative plan that works for everyone involved. It's not good enough to just say, "Sorry, I can't do that." You always need to make your best effort at finding an alternative value to replace your original commitment.

If I commit a specific discount to a customer and then determine that I can't provide that discount as anticipated, I then have to search for other areas in which I can add value. Maybe I can provide extended payment terms, free education through work with a partner, or some free consultation with my teammates and me. People often understand when things have to change, provided you make a serious effort to offer something else of value.

The same goes for time commitments; if it turns out that you cannot honor a time commitment, inform the affected parties as early as possible. "If you ignore it long enough, it will go away" doesn't work. When you ignore a situation that you should be addressing immediately, it will only worsen with time. Recall the Fram Oil Filter commercial's statement: "Pay me now or pay me later." That statement holds true, and typically, the later payment comes with interest.

When you consider making commitments, there are two important questions you need to ask yourself. The first question needs to be "Can I realistically meet this commitment if I make it"? If the answer to that question is not a resounding yes, then you probably shouldn't make the commitment. I am a bit of a risk taker, but when it comes to making a commitment to a customer, I am quite careful and thoughtful about what I am committing to and to whom I am committing it. Prior to putting my reputation on the line or putting my team, company, or myself on the hook for the commitment, I am going to weigh both the responsibility and the risk, should I fail to deliver as promised.

The second question you should ask yourself is "Have I properly and clearly communicated precisely what and when I will deliver on this commitment?" In other words, have you properly set expectations with the customer so there is absolutely no question about the commitment? It doesn't hurt to revisit expectations with clients at various intervals, just in case changes have occurred in their thought processes that they have not shared with you. Also, if you do have to modify commitments, doing so early enough to enable expectations to be properly managed is very important. In a situation where your contact is someone who will then have to manage the expectations of others within an organization, it is best to provide the contact with as much notice as possible.

In summary, don't overcommit and don't ever assume that the other person understands what you are saying.

FOLLOW THROUGH

Paying attention to details and then making sure everything is complete have always been important, but their importance cannot be overstated especially in today's business world. Because companies are often heavily scrutinized, it is important to establish processes and procedures that provide checks and balances. Making sure that all requirements are carried out as early as possible will likely prevent delays or derailments later in the sales cycle. Through experience, you probably know very well by now that there are no shortcuts; to ensure that a transaction will be completed, nothing may be eliminated from the diligence of the process. Following through rigorously on the finalization of all required steps will generate momentum and positive habits that will pay huge dividends.

DELIVER WHAT YOU SELL

Integrity is the single most positive attribute that a salesperson can possess. Without it, all the skill in the world will not sustain success over an extended period of time. Integrity has lasting value. A deal by itself is only as valuable as the impact it has on the current quota. When next year comes, the deal made this year loses much, if not all, of its value.

Delivering what you sell means making sure that you get clients what they need on time. It also means that you are accurately representing the capabilities of your products and services.

Beyond that, delivering on your commitments to your partners is also important. Some will refer to partners as vendors; I prefer not to see them in that limited way. Instead I view them and treat them as collaborators, which connotes that they are truly part of our business. To take full advantage of your partners' capabilities you must build and maintain close, trusting, and inclusive relationships with them.

When it comes time to delivering what you sell to clients, you have to depend on and assist both your internal and external partners with the delivery of their portions. That is why I recommend that you have jointly developed processes, joint planning, joint training, and joint marketing and selling efforts. It is incumbent upon you and your company to teach your partners what your clients' needs and expectations are as well as what you have committed to deliver. By doing this you will also develop tighter relationships with partners and thus become more capable of helping your clients. In the process you will be able to more effectively leverage your partners in the sales cycle, to provide evident value to your prospects. That partnership bond will impress your clients and provide you with a relationship that will extend your virtual team both on the delivery side and the commercial side of your business.

FOLLOW UP

Part of managing your partners to help you deliver what you sell is making sure things go as they should during the selling process. If a customer needs technical education, a statement-of-work (SOW) explanation, or delivery parameters, whether they are coming from someone other than your internal organization or within your company, you need to make certain that the client's needs are met. If a client has any questions about their order or potential order, you must make sure those questions are answered in a timely manner.

If there are changes to be made on delivery address, customer business name, configuration, or shipping date, you need to follow up to make certain that those changes are completed accurately and on time. You then must communicate back to the customer and to your partner (if applicable) any pertinent information that will ensure a successful transaction.

When it comes to follow up, the buck always stops right on your doorstep, Sales Professional!

COMMUNICATE

So how do you not assume anything and still feel comfortable that your customer knows exactly what to expect, even when something may have changed? You communicate! The critical importance of communicating is addressed in "Selling through Leadership."

Did you know that studies show the number-one factor for success is communication skills?

Effective communication is probably your single most controllable and important aspect of working with prospects and clients. There is no replacement for communication. When I am waiting to receive something or hear from someone and I am getting the silent treatment, I begin to get nervous about the outcome. The other reaction I sometimes have when others delay communicating with me is that they really aren't all that interested in doing business with me.

Through the years I have learned a few things about communication that I feel are important. One is that if I am prospecting or selling to a customer and I don't communicate with them, someone else will. Because communication is so important, it could make the difference between winning or losing a deal or even getting an opportunity to participate in the customer's buying process. There is no acceptable excuse for not communicating; the benefits far outweigh the effort required to appropriately and effectively stay in touch. Making a call or writing an e-mail are little things that can make a big difference.

Some clients will prefer speaking to you, while others prefer using e-mail or text. A deal can sometimes be accomplished over the phone, but some clients want to see a person before buying from her or him. Do the very best you can to honor your customer's preferred method of communication.

My personal favorite method of communication is to be in front of the customer. I find that really good things happen when I can meet face-to-face. If your business doesn't allow you to always be in front of the customer, you have to be innovative and make the best of your budgeted funds and time to communicate effectively. Some people don't return phone calls consistently; those people probably prefer that you communicate via e-mail. I am still catching myself from time to time as I realize that clients are returning my phone calls via e-mail. The purpose of communication is to build rapport with customers so that you can be as informed as possible of their needs, goals, and motivations. Without that level of understanding you cannot possibly optimize your value to them.

Those who know me well know that I am a stickler for communication. None of us is the perfect communicator, but all of us can get better at it. There is absolutely no acceptable substitute for communicating. Communication is key!

FORECAST ACCURATELY

Forecasting your business and doing it accurately is critically important to the short-term and long-term health of your business (territory), your profit and loss statements (P&L), and your company. Forecasting begins with you and each individual deal you make, but it affects the entire company. What you forecast doesn't necessarily stop when it gets to your sales management, your division management, or your top management. If you work for a public entity, it may also be included in your company's annual reports or SEC filings. So whenever you may be feeling insignificant in the grand scheme of things, you just need to remember how important each deal forecast is to your entire company and its stockholders.

Beyond the ramifications for your business and investors, your forecasting accuracy is tremendously important to your sales leader and to your product and operations managers for headcount, product-development investing, and training purposes. All of these growth plans typically result from business projections and profitability. If your company is not meeting your projections, you will likely have to cut back on spending. If you are not making what the business needs to sustain all its necessary functions, jobs could be at stake, research-and-development (R&D) funding could suffer, critical marketing presence could diminish, and support and implementation staffing and necessary tools could be reduced.

Forecasting figures in all of the above critical business implications, and it also provides dramatic benefit to you in terms of knowing your deals, knowing your clients, and managing your territories. Accurate forecasting takes more than a "dartboard" approach or a best-guess effort. To accurately forecast business, you must first know the prospective business and then be close to the pulse of that opportunity. If you are following guidelines and staying close to your business opportunities, you will not only be better informed, but better able to positively affect business outcomes.

Being close to the business allows you to always know where you stand with a particular deal and with your territory in general. The bottom line is that it is better to know than to guess.

Forecasting—that is, using a forecasting rhythm and system—should be mandatory in any business environment, so why not take advantage of its capability and do it well? The benefits will once again far outweigh the required effort. Accurate forecasting, like communicating, is key!

Personal Development

Personal development is only important if you want to continue living and growing and learning and achieving. You are gifted with a unique potential that can define your destiny provided you seek to reach that potential. You can quickly determine if you are really where you want to be or have done all that you want to do by asking yourself these five questions:

1) What do you like about yourself?
2) What do you wish was different about your life or you?
3) What are your hopes in life, that is, your true dreams?
4) How would you describe your own unique potential?
5) What do you need to do to learn to accept and appreciate the things in your life that you can't change?

There is no man living who isn't capable of doing more than he thinks he can do.

—HENRY FORD

SIX THINGS YOU MUST DO TO REACH THE TOP IN SALES

1. MAKE THINGS HAPPEN

Some of us thrive on making things happen. Others of us prefer to just let things happen and respond when required to respond. Are the results the same? Perhaps in rare instances they are. In most cases, though, being proactive versus reactive will produce far greater value. Being proactive requires some courage and forethought. Forethought is always a positive occurrence if it does not become a deterrent to taking good initiative. Proactive thinkers and doers normally see the glass half-full, so forward thinking is usually a part of the makeup of those people. Reactive thinkers are more pessimistic and often see the glass as half-empty.

What is the connection between proactivity and forward thinking? Proactive people most often are also willing to take an occasional risk. With that, they also exhibit some courage and know that they may encounter some adversity, criticism, jealousy, or procedural obstacle.

Most salespeople do not like cold calling. Fear of rejection becomes an obstacle for them. The obstacle can be overcome in a number of ways, beginning with the notion that there is really no such thing as a completely cold call. I covered that concept in "Professionalism," but it has resonance for personal development as well. Two major factors can always be kept in mind when you are making the cold call:

a. If you have done some research, you know something about the company and person whom you are calling.

b. You are only trying to help the prospect company, and there need be no risk or fear associated with wanting to do the right thing.

Great people, such as those who are willing to take the chill out of the cold call, have a common view of obstacles. They see them as motivators and opportunities for success.

I thank God for my handicaps, for through them,
I have found myself, my work, and my God.

—HELEN KELLER

Problems are only opportunities in work clothes.

—HENRY J. KAISER

Think of the enormous obstacles that Helen Keller overcame to become great. She was not resigned to being blind, deaf, and mute. She wanted to strive for her unique potential. Imagine yourself in her position at an early age, and ask yourself what you would have done.

I have talked a fair amount over the years about being a leader versus a follower. You don't have to be a manager or the captain of your soccer team or the chairperson of a committee to be a leader. The fact is that some managers aren't great leaders, and some leaders are not interested in or particularly adept at the administrative rigors required of management.

Always remember this: you and I lead by asking the best of others and ourselves. By doing so, we truly make things happen.

And why wait to make things happen? Don't procrastinate, because if you do you may one day hear yourself say something like this, "That was my idea a long time ago, and now my colleague is getting all the credit for doing it." Don't be fooled into thinking that "letting things happen" and "making things happen" will render similar results.

2. PUT MORE INTO YOUR TIME

Earlier I wrote about the importance of time management and how you enrich your life by managing your time instead of letting it manage you. I also wrote about prioritizing in relation to time management. I suggested using a simple goal list as an aid in that process. Making use of a simple goal list will help protect an asset that is given to us all but lost if it is not used.

In other words, time is something you can't get back once it ticks away. If you waste time, it is wasted indeed. While scientists may continue to attempt to create time machines, as far as I know, only God has the capability to go back in time. There is no "undo" function available when it comes to time, unless of course, you or someone you know has a time machine at your disposal. Then you can take advantage—as arrogant, self-indulgent Phil (Bill Murray) did in the movie *Groundhog Day*—of opportunities to relive a certain day until you get it right. If you ever discover how to make that happen, you know how to reach me. Please call at any time of night or day!

When you get the greatest possible ROI (return on investment) of time, you have optimized your satisfaction with your management of the precious commodity. Doing so will require effort and thought about what you want to achieve. Remember, if you don't manage your own time, someone who is really only concerned about managing his or her own time will do it for you.

Make your time count. You have only one opportunity to make the best of a particular moment in time, and then it will be gone forever. In the context of selling, one way to make the most of your time is to put more into it. You can do that in several ways, starting with doing a job that you really like. Another way is to learn all that you can and never stop learning. That way you will have abundant knowledge to go along with your great wisdom about a topic and about the people you work with, and you will be able to serve as a true professional.

Learning to negotiate is an enriching exercise for a salesperson. Learning to negotiate with clients will flow nicely into negotiating with both internal and external partners. Also, learning to negotiate will benefit your personal life outside of work. Do you ever stop negotiating? If so, you had better be content with being a doormat.

Strategic Negotiations (Dietmeyer and Kaplan) provides a guidance system that offers commonsense principles and strategies that, when applied to the field of business negotiations, will revolutionize the process as you know it. You may learn a lot and benefit highly by reading the book and applying its principles, one of which is to "create joint value" between your customer and you. Without joint value you do not have the possibility of a win-win situation.

Putting more into your time requires you to be willing to look at your situation and yourself and to not only submit to change, but be committed to change. Expecting different results without changing is essentially a pipe dream. Reaching greatness in your individual life or as a team requires something more and other than what you are accustomed to doing.

We must be willing to let go of the life we planned so as to have the life that is waiting for us.

—JOSEPH CAMPBELL

Ask yourself the following questions. I suggest you write down the answers.

1) What prevents you from taking hold of what is important and what needs to be done?
2) What is an issue that you are dealing with right now?
3) When you think about this issue, what do you need to take hold of?
4) What do you need to let go of regarding this issue?
5) How does taking hold versus letting go connect with your ability to fulfill your unique potential?

3. DITCH THE EXCUSES

I wrote earlier about turning obstacles into opportunities and about taking risks. Both concepts are easy enough to intellectualize, but equally difficult to internalize. The reason is that we humans generally have a fear of failure and perhaps a fear of success as well. I personally get confused at times about what is holding me back, or perhaps more to the point, what I am holding onto that is keeping me back.

Believe it or not, work is one of my favorite excuses. I've been heard to say things like "I'm not as fit as I would like to be because I work long hours and haven't the time to work out as much as I need to." Or I say, "I haven't gone back to school for my second master's degree, in marketing, because of spending way too much time at work." And I have often said, "I don't use all of my vacation time because work is way too demanding, and I can't get away." I love those excuses. I use them all the time. My son Bradley's response to any of them would simply be "That's rubbish!"

Here is one of my favorite quotes. It applies to taking risks and striving to reach our unique potential: "The greatest danger for most of us is not that our aim is too high and we miss it, but that it is too low and we reach it" (Michelangelo).

Being afraid of failing is one of my biggest liabilities in life. I hate to fail as much as I hate to lose. It is a good thing that Abraham Lincoln was not afraid to fail. Or was he? Whether he had been unafraid of failure or had simply faced his fears head on, the results were the same.

We all must first fail before we can truly grow. That is a difficult concept to grasp, but give it sincere consideration, and you will soon discover that you have learned the most through your failures. There is something about failing that motivates many of us... if ever we are going to be motivated. Some people, of course, never become motivated to change by failure and fall into a pattern of one failure after another. I have a great deal of sympathy for those who victimize themselves in that way and wish them success at breaking their own mold and finding their unique potential in life. Ironically, those who never risk failure are failing to grow and not benefitting from that failure, either.

Failure is a better teacher than success, but she seldom finds an apple on her desk.

—ANONYMOUS

When I grab hold of an idea and let go of the outcome, I am almost always rewarded. I believe I am rewarded because I tried. Whether or not my idea or effort becomes a success is not nearly as important as the fact that I had the courage to give it a try. Finding that courage and daring to have a go at it were my rewards, and they enabled me to try again and again. Essentially I learned how to get out of my comfort zone—in which I allowed myself to be uncomfortable—and into the game. Try seeking out your courage; you may also grow to like it. Start today by discovering your number-one excuse and ditching it!

4. GET TRAINING DONE WITH ENTHUSIASM
Training can be burdensome and sometimes seem overwhelming. With increasing industry regulations and changing codes of ethics, compliance standards have continued to increase during my tenure in the workforce. Over the years I have felt the need to develop training programs for various internal teams and have given the programs names like Sales Academy of Excellence and 2.5x (two point five x) Training. Participating in such programs while also staying abreast of industry-expertise requirements can become very time-consuming. It is truly difficult to keep up. Because of the potential downside of the training burden, I think the value of training is worth a look. I believe you should be thankful for such opportunities to learn. As you strive to improve your performance and grow your expertise, training plays a critical role and can't always be effectively replaced by practical experience. This is true particularly if you are constrained by extensive travel and have a well-defined job to perform each day; getting practical experience that parallels something new that you would otherwise train for requires too much time and distracts too much from the completion of day-to-day work. Therefore, condensed and

intensive training sessions may be best for meeting or supplementing your overall training needs.

Many companies spend a great deal of money on training because they understand the importance of knowing the business and the products being sold. Other companies provide little formal training, which leaves its employees to seek outside training programs. Whatever situation you find yourself in, do your best to get the most from all training in which you can participate. By constantly striving to improve, you will apply rigor, synergy, and conscience (explained below) to training and as a result will attain maximum benefit.

Training should not be viewed as vacation; the two should never be confused. While away at training, it is critical to maintain full attendance. You only retain a certain percentage of what you are taught anyway, so if you further reduce that percentage by absenteeism, you not only cheat yourself, but you cheat your team and your company. Rigor with regard to training needs to be your prime motivator when you are granted the privilege of furthering your knowledge and increasing your value.

Synergy refers to what team members do to help one another. When you train, maintain synergy by pulling on the TEAM (Together Everyone Achieves More) rope. Since we need others to be successful ourselves, we should all help each other get more out of the training provided. So you need to do your best at training to help not only yourself but also your teammates to be the best in the business.

Conscience is that inner voice that should be reminding you to give it your best shot and that says that your team and your company are depending on you. You are depending on you, too. Through training, you often can achieve more within your profession.

Inspiration is very important on those training days when the work is piling up around you and you feel the pressure to meet a demand from someone else, be it a customer, a peer, or management. It is particularly difficult on those days to find the inspiration to stay in the training seat, remain focused on the training, and do the best you can when your mind is elsewhere. That is when another aspect of teamwork becomes important. The concept of Brother's Keeper then becomes a key component of your individual and collective success. Brother's Keeper is simply about helping others reach their best. Sometimes Brother's Keeper gets confused with negative terms such as "ratting out" someone, but it should never get to that point. Holding people accountable to be their best takes courage and genuine concern. Ratting someone out is often an illustration of the absence of courage and a motivation to see them fail. Rather than lovingly discussing concerns about perceived poor performance with a fellow employee, ratting them out to a superior is often an effort to hurt them versus help them.

> *Our chief want is someone who will inspire us to be what we know we could be.*
>
> —RALPH WALDO EMERSON

Not everyone will agree with Emerson's statement, but I know that I personally need help from my friends and teammates to get or remain inspired enough to do a quality, effective job. Sometimes that inspiration comes in the form of encouraging words. Sometimes that inspiration comes from being called out on something that has me off track. We all get off track from time to time and need to have attitude and action adjustments to get us moving back in the right direction.

> *A person often meets his destiny on the road he took to avoid it.*
>
> —JEAN DE LA FONTAINE

This saying reminds me that there are times when I have a bad attitude or am off track and want to stay there. It sometimes takes the courage and caring of another person to help me adjust and get healthy again. Ask yourself these questions, and perhaps write down the answers. Then read them again, and think about what they mean to you.

- When have you inspired yourself with your courage and risk taking?
- Where and when have members of your team inspired you?
- What are your deepest dreams and your vision for yourself?
- Is there an area of your life where you are playing small or have essentially lowered your self-expectations? Explain.
- Do you feel worthy to inspire others?
- How might you liberate yourself from fear to liberate others?

Inspiration should be job number one in your life. Seek to be inspired and to inspire others. Brother's Keeper is a concept that requires courageous and caring inspiration to and for your teammates and yourself. If you think someone is off track, please call them on it. If you are called out, you have an obligation to (1) take your job seriously and (2) if the shoe fits wear it, but if not, throw it away. Your team should always be a safe place to practice Brother's Keeper and to be held to your best. It is all for the good of the gang and every person that is part of it. If your organization or a team or other subgroup of it is not a safe place in which to grow, there are leadership issues that need to be addressed and altered to make it a safe place.

5. WHEN TIMES ARE GOOD, ACCELERATE!

I am going to begin this topic with a statement that may seem a bit negative. You never really "arrive" in business or life. You will never be perfect. That is an easy one to explain. None of us is flawless, and you can count more on not becoming flawless in this life than you can on having to pay taxes. But guess what? There is not much that you can do about that. You can try and try, and you should try and try, but you will never reach perfection.

In your job as a professional salesperson, you have a quota. Your quota is annually established, so regardless of how you do this year, whenever your new fiscal year kicks off, you begin at 0 percent or zero dollars. Therefore, you never really arrive except for a brief time at most. That doesn't mean you can't win all the time and get to 100-plus percent each year.

> *Winning isn't everything; it's the only thing.*
>
> —WIDELY ATTRIBUTED TO VINCE LOMBARDI
> (QUOTING RED SAUNDERS)

I borrowed that phrase from Lombardi and Saunders, but I attach a slightly different meaning to it than those sports figures did. To me, you can always find a win in every situation. Even with regard to a loss on paper, you can find something to help you win or gain something from the situation. When I was a soccer coach, for example, I always looked for the wins in losses, because I believed that there had to be something in the losses that would have positive effects on us. Even if that win was as minor as working hard and never quitting, it was considered and talked about as a win that we could build success from.

> *Success is never final and failure never fatal. It's*
> *courage that counts.*
>
> —ATTRIBUTED TO GEORGE TILTON

> *In every negative situation there is an upside.*
> *Finding it is like finding gold.*
>
> —ANONYMOUS

If the above statements are true, why take your foot off the accelerator in either prosperous or lean times? Success is never final, and failure is never fatal. When you are doing well, you should never relax, because you could become complacent, uninspired, lazy, or otherwise likely to derail your success.

Bad habits can eventually become arthritic, so always try to stay away from them, even when times are really good and it appears you can coast a bit. You should continue to overplan, overprepare, overpractice, and be very consistent with your rigor in the sales process. Make use of all the accelerative power that resides in your DNA.

Brian A Mitchell

6. HANG AROUND WITH WINNERS

Good habits beget good habits. Momentum is a fascinating force. As an athlete, coach, and salesperson, I have seen and experienced incredible swings in momentum. As shown above, I advise against letting off the accelerator when times are good because I think momentum swings often result from doing just that. When I have been ahead in games or matches and let up a bit, the next thing I knew, my team was in battle and sometimes would lose because of it. As a coach, one of my most frustrating experiences was helplessly watching my team lose a playoff soccer match after having a 2–0 lead and owning the run of play for well into the second half of the game. We let off mentally; the other team sensed it and gained confidence enough to catapult itself to victory. Momentum is powerful and can be as painful as it is pleasurable.

One of my favorite momentum stories was about playing a match in the Cape Cod Soccer League. My team played miserably the entire first half and trailed 3–0. In the second half we came out working very hard and began to sense a shift in the run of play. We scored at about the seventy-three-minute mark to cut the margin to 3–1. We gained a bit of confidence from that and continued to battle. With eight minutes remaining, we scored again to cut the margin to 3–2. Just prior to that, I collided with an upright, and blocked a certain goal that would have put the match out of reach. My team and I both became very fired up by my dangerous effort.

As time wound down we continued to press hard, and one of the most brilliant individual plays that I have ever witnessed drew us level with about two seconds remaining in regulation. Jackie Brown, our left-winger from Tufts University, amazed us all with a brilliant and deft display of individual dribbling and composure to nestle the tie goal into the back of the other team's net as time was expiring. During overtime, it was all us, and we won the match 4–3 in the single greatest comeback that I have ever played in. I still get chills when I think about that Sunday afternoon when I was nineteen years old.

The lesson learned in both these situations was simple: don't let off the accelerator, and negative momentum will probably never take over.

Successful people are often very consistent with their work rate, their habits, and their rigor. They can inspire us by just being around them. It is excellent advice when someone encourages us to hang around with overachievers and to stay away from underachievers. Just as momentum swings can win or lose matches, they can have both positive and negative effects on our lives and our work.

Hanging around with peacemakers versus troublemakers is also good advice. There is plenty of trouble in this world and in our workplaces without trying to find or stir up more. We should, of course, stand up for what is right with conviction and rigor, but to cause trouble where no trouble is warranted is a waste of time, energy, and goodwill.

The same holds true for negative talk or gossip. With ever-increasing workloads and pressure to perform well, we should not be able to find time to gossip. I find gossiping to be one of my most frequent negative-behavior tendencies. My most humbling experiences stem from when I realize that I am gossiping. Nothing good comes from gossiping, and hanging around with gossips is not a healthy habit.

Overachievers more frequently focus on helping others rather than tearing them down. There are many ways you can do that, as I have illustrated with Brother's Keeper and with the practice of seeking unique potential in others as well as us.

Early Capital One credit-card advertisements remind me of a behavior that you should not practice. In those commercials the word "no" was used so often that nothing positive ever got accomplished (until one signed up with Capital One, of course). I believe that if you are always saying no or displaying an "it's not my job" attitude, you can become a detriment to success for both your company and yourself. The word no can also gain momentum within a team and a company and can be like the proverbial bad apple.

Of course, saying no is necessary when trying to avoid over-commitments and denying or rejecting incorrect information. Tempering no with alternatives, suggestions, or other forms of help can really take the sting out of the word and leave in its place a positive perception. When negotiating, no to a wish-list request most often needs to be said in an entirely different way so as to offer a positive alternative.

Truth over harmony is a concept that can become an amazingly liberating concept when put into practice. Self-truth and truth with others are both incredibly valuable in your growth process. Our youngest child, Patrick, attended a private high school that focused on character education in Bath, Maine, where truth over harmony is practiced daily. Most of us who were involved in this education program found the principle extremely difficult to put into practice. As humans our natural tendency is to prefer to get along or get by and not address the sometimes-difficult truths before us. It is so often easier to ignore a situation than to address it head on. When we do address the truth, it can make us miserable for a time, but it ultimately will set us free.

> *All truths are easy to understand once they are*
> *discovered; the point is to discover them.*
>
> —Galileo

Try answering these questions and see what they reveal to you:

1) Describe an important lesson you learned in adolescence or early childhood that involved telling the truth. How did it change you?
2) How honest are you today with your team or leadership associates?
3) If you had a major life issue, would you tend to share it or keep it from your team or leadership associates?
4) When have you inspired yourself with your honesty?
5) Is there a truth about your potential, purpose, or destiny that you have been avoiding?

The bottom line is that it is excellent habit to hang around with people who inspire you in a positive way and not a negative way. In addition, participating in or attending inspirational speaking, reading, music, and service to others are all ways to develop momentum that can turn into habits that can enrich your life.

For me, staying on track requires continuous effort. If I get off track, I must make immediate adjustments. The rigor in my effort, the synergy in my understanding of my surroundings, my clients, and my teammates, and the voice speaking in my ear telling me to do what is right are all part of my seeking to reach my unique potential as a professional salesperson. I never will arrive, but if I continue to strive for my best and get help from my friends along the way, I will get closer by the minute.

We all have ideal statuses we want to achieve or ideal persons we want to become. If we didn't, we would be living in a complete vacuum without feelings, desires, or goals of any sort. The difference between where a person is and where a person wants to be is her or his own personal gap. We all have gaps, and the way we can close them is illustrated by the "How?" graphic below. The process applies to all aspects of life and all people, regardless of position, talent, or level of inspiration. In the context of a commercial vocation (sales and marketing), the depicted "Inspiration + Execution" equation represents both wanting to accomplish something (becoming or doing) and taking action. Courage to get into the game is required, and then staying in the game, doing what is needed, and realizing some gain or improvement in closing the gap are what make the process continue. Momentum is critical, and continuous improvement is the reward. Vince Lombardi used to say, "Perfection is not attainable, but if we chase perfection we can catch excellence."

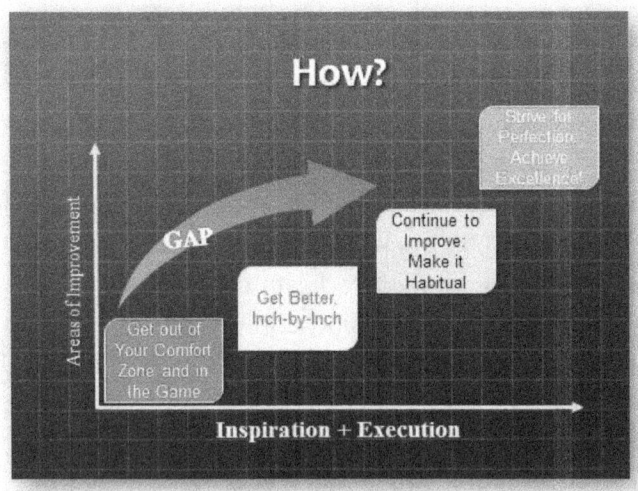

Closing the Gap 1

To assist with the process of getting into the game of continuous improvement and closing the gap between where you are today and where you want to be, or better yet who you are today and who you want to become, I have included four additional success habits to help you get there.

Think about the topics and then apply them to your personal and work lives to hopefully help you become who you want to be so to accomplish that which you desire to accomplish.

1. ALWAYS DO MORE THAN EXPECTED OF YOU

As industry leaders, whether managers or not, we are all challenged by performance expectations. This first of the four success habits in this chapter addresses the topic of performance from a nontechnical perspective.

Let's begin with what we expect of ourselves and work backward. Do we expect ourselves to come into the day/week/situation with a fresh perspective? That could include a can-do attitude, an innovative thought process, or a determination to find a better way. It could be that we are determined to manage time better, prepare more thoroughly for meetings, or manage expectations better by being thoughtful and communicating like a pro. There are a number of ways in which we can improve today, even if only a smidgen. So what are our expectations of ourselves? Is this just another dreaded day like many Mondays, or a day on which we intend to make a positive difference for those around us and in so doing, improve ourselves as well?

Our hearts could be heavy for some reason, and we may feel drained. That makes it difficult for us to be upbeat and energized at work. We may be facing a fearful situation that saps us emotionally and drives our stress level skyward. Whatever it is, we will have to struggle through the day, not to mention be a positive leader and make others feel good about themselves while helping them with their success. Today, maybe doing more than expected is simply doing that—in our difficulty, remaining a servant leader for others, or someone who tries to help those around us, including our clients and patients, to attain their best.

It may be only the little things today that help us do more than expected. The big ideas, bold moves, exceptional energy, and jovial attitude may not get released. That is OK as long as we remember (1) we are privileged to lead and (2) leading brings with it a responsibility for maintaining irrepressible optimism. If we do only these two things today, they themselves will allow us to exceed expectations.

2. MAINTAIN A POSITIVE ATTITUDE

Did you ever end your week by saying, "What happened to the week? It flew by, didn't it? Man, I didn't complete half of what I intended to. I had such a good plan. But then she wanted this, and he wanted that, and they dragged me into meetings that were not on my calendar, and that potential partner of mine didn't call me back as promised and really ticked me off! I am so glad the weekend is near. I need a break. A vacation would be perfect right now. Ah heck! I've already taken my vacation. Sometimes I feel like packing up the old SUV with my tent, hiking boots, and bike, and heading for the mountains!"

Sound at all familiar? If so, don't feel alone, because you are in the company of thousands, if not millions of people who likely say something similar every week.

My wish for you is that your Friday this week is different from the one described in the previous paragraph and is yet another happy Friday. It should be, after all, right? You had five days to accomplish a great deal—a significant list of goals for the week. Going to a game or watching one on TV, having dinner at a friend's house, getting together with family after church for an old-fashioned Sunday dinner. What a life! Thus, it should be easy to maintain a positive attitude, but is it?

This habit of successful people sometimes can feel like we are trying to get those words out with a mouth full of marbles. It somehow just doesn't flow as the words in the first paragraph did. So today we want solutions to the challenge we often have to maintain a positive attitude. At the Global Leadership Summit that I attended in 2012, Condoleezza Rice stated that as leaders we have a major responsibility to be "irrepressible optimists." That is not just a temporary feeling or a quick re-minder—it is to be a condition or state of being that we live in, day after day after day. As leaders we are to consider it an honor and an absolute privilege to be in a position of leader-ship. And why shouldn't we? If we have the spirit of leadership within us, it then becomes our responsibility to realize that we are gifted and blessed by that spirit and that we have a respon-sibility to never accept the world as it is but push to get it to where we think it should be.

Let's stop right there for a moment and think about that last sentence. We have been gifted or blessed, and we have the responsibility or must do what we can to make things better. How awesome is that? Suddenly my week wasn't so bad after all. Ms. Rice also said, "Consider it a privilege to struggle." That rang a bell with me because I am a huge proponent of that idea. If we want to continuously improve or get better, we need to get out of our comfort zone and get in the game, right? Is that always easy? No! So we struggle to get there, but then when we make gains, we feel good about it, and we gain momentum. Sometimes we feel really good or even great about those wins.

So, how is your attitude doing today? Are you irrepressibly optimistic even though things didn't go 100 percent your way this week? If they didn't go all your way what did you learn from the experience? I was supposed to have attended a second day of that Global Leadership Summit, but I didn't. I paid for it and planned on it, but because I had other things to accomplish that I believed more important, I stayed put in my office to accomplish those other goals. But, just that short period of time spent with Condoleezza Rice was an inspiration for which I am thankful and continue to hold fast to as time marches forward.

Just for a moment, let's go back to the topic of attitude and what I wrote in an earlier paragraph. All of the unplanned inter-ruptions I had and the "irresponsible" partner who didn't call me back—what did I learn from them? Thinking about it, the calls that I received might not have occurred if I had delegat-ed authority to my team instead of delegating tasks. When it comes down to it, delegating tasks creates followers, not lead-ers. Giving authority and then trusting my team will make them better leaders. I believe I just learned something from a "less than perfect" week. At that same GLS, I heard Jim Collins say that "great leaders get high returns from bad events." So just maybe—if I had been a real leader instead of a task delegator—I would not have had my plan turned so upside down. OK, now I know, and you know what? I feel pretty darned good about my mistake! That's right. I blew it but feel good about it because I just learned from it. You might say that I "failed forward" be-cause of the way that I used the losses of the week to win. Next!

Remember, if you're not dead, you're not done

3. WORK WITH ENTHUSIASM

This topic seems as if it is an obvious bullet point that needs no explanation. Perhaps so, but let's explore a little together anyway. What does it really mean to work with enthusiasm? One might begin by saying that it is working hard, working with fervor, or having a positive attitude all the time. Those are certainly good habits on the surface. Let's see if we can take it to another level and examine how going deeper and broader may add even more value to working with enthusiasm. Answer these five questions for yourself.

- Are you working as an enthusiastic learner, continuously trying to improve in all areas of work and in dealing with others?
- Do you maintain an external focus by keeping an eye on the industry, anticipating changes, and generally looking around corners and ahead for future developments that could affect your business, workflow, or competitive requirements?
- Do you use your imagination to do a better job or to help others do theirs?
- Are you inclusive in your thoughts and decision-making process by asking others for advice, opinion, comments, or suggestions and treating them as if their ideas matter?
- Are you distinguishing between effort and results by working smarter versus working harder?

Answering these questions can begin to reveal whether or not you are really working with enthusiasm. I believe that working with enthusiasm goes beyond working hard or long—it extends to becoming better at what we do and helping those around us do the same. In today's viciously competitive business climate, we just can't expect status quo to be good enough. Looking for that "edge" is something that we should always be alert to doing.

Think about these things for three minutes or so each and then take two more minutes to make some notes to yourself about how you answered these five questions. I will be curious to know what thoughts you generated.

Here's to working with enthusiasm!

4. FIND A MENTOR

There is nothing uncommon about having a need for a mentor, teacher, role model, or sage adviser to turn to when in times of need. They can be a very valuable part of our lives—better still, if we make our mentors an integral part of our ongoing "continuous-improvement" effort. The question becomes—whether you do this on a regular, open-minded, and seeking basis. To do so, you first have to have some measure of courage or a sense of self-security and self-confidence to release you from that self-restrictive inner wiring that often says no to seeking help.

Speaking personally, I know fully the cage in which we can find ourselves. Stepping out of our comfort zone (as it has been for me—over and over again) is often the only way to break free of the self-inflicted chains in which we bind ourselves. First we have to discover that we are bound. With that realization, we can begin to determine to change our situation by getting into the game of self-improvement through various ways, including a mentoring or role model relationship.

Notice how often I used the word "self" in the first two para-graphs. It was to make the point that I get in my own way. I can make many excuses, find abundant justification, and develop in-tellectual rationalizations about making it OK to point the finger elsewhere, but at the end of the day—I am he who gets in the way of me.

Some find it easy and comfortable to seek advice. We likely learned that it was a good thing from Mom, Dad, Grandmother, Grandfather, or a wonderful teacher from our younger days. Others, like me, find it difficult. For those who find it easy—if you don't already have a mentor or role-model relationship, what are you waiting for? Are you being complacent (perhaps lazy)? You can't possibly believe that you have all the wisdom there is to have. You are much too bright for that!

For those of us who find it difficult to seek and build such relationships (without exploring all the reasons why), let's just say that for some of us, seeking mentoring was an admission of defi-ciency. Wow!

When perfection is all we want to be known for, seeking to correct a deficiency is a difficult path to follow. In fact, it could become very revealing and painful. So how then can we begin in spite of our fear? How can we step out into the uncomfort-able world of vulnerability? What if we begin with something less difficult, less public, and more between me and myself? One of the ways I found it less difficult to essentially tackle myself was through books and, believe it or not, movies. I have my favorite books and authors, and I have my favorite heroes, both real and fictional. With the encouragement of these tools and the desires of my heart to become more and better, I have been able to be-come more open to asking for sage advice and help. I guess you

Brian A Mitchell

could say that I gained the ability to trust others with my life story and my life challenges. Thank God! I have often said that we have one thing in common—none of us is perfect. We also have a second thing in common—we all need to be loved. It isn't easy to be vulnerable unless we feel safe. Providing safety for someone is about loving that person enough to commit to being safe for him or her.

As a bit of an aside, I have often talked about the concept of "Brother's Keeper." Not necessarily a mentoring role, but very similar, this practice can draw teams closer, help them be more effective, and provide a growth environment unlike most. The idea is to care enough to hold one another to our best. The keys are (1) to know each other and (2) to care for each other. Example: Jeff determines that I am being a bit careless about describing the IT infrastructure at SPi as "Yeah, we have the usual production environment and some DR and backup process in place." If really we have an innovative, application-aware DR system that is unique in our space, I am not telling the truth well. If Jeff ever hears the former from me, what might he think? How might he feel about a teammate saying this? And more important, he will surely realize that I am not putting our best foot forward to the person to whom I am speaking. So if Jeff cares enough about me and knows of my good intentions, he will take me aside and let me know that he believes in my best and "didn't hear it" when I made that comment. I will, I hope, thank Jeff for his care and concern for me and commit mentally and in my heart to do a better job next time. Brother's Keeper is a proven practice to help build strong leaders and better performers.

My role models today include authors whom I believe—and savor the wisdom they offer; western movie characters (that's right); an old evangelist, an old gentleman who calls me "Young

Brian," a personal coach, a former high school principal (now deceased) who once kicked my butt in front of the entire girls' basketball team, and of course God himself. From each I continue to receive revelations (some painful), encouragement, wisdom, inspiration, and motivation. They are all part of my personal mentor program and my continuous-improvement process.

So we can all be well advised to always keep in touch with the books, the movies, and the people who widen our horizon and make it possible for us to stretch ourselves.

Planning

The reason most people never reach their goals is that they don't define them or ever seriously consider them as believable or achievable. Winners can tell you where they are going, what they plan to do along the way, and who will be sharing the adventure with them.

—Denis Waitley, *The Psychology of Winning*

Former fighter pilot Ed Rush's book, *Fighter Pilot Performance*, provided me with some interesting insight into the planning process. He gave me the idea that our plans should be like missions (in fighter-pilot terms). They should be broken down simply and then executed promptly and efficiently. Planning is imperative for us to reach our goals, mission, vision, and values in life, both at work and home, so think of a mission as a project or significant task that needs to be completed. Plans are something that you should build for each mission that you have. Plans are also something that you should consider dynamic versus static, to be reviewed and not put on the shelf, to be a work in progress and not a finished product.

Rush describes the mission this way:

1. Fight your way to the target.
2. Drop your bombs.
3. Fight your way home.

Of course, planning any mission is not quite as simple as this three-step process may make it seem, but I like the idea of taking as much complication as possible out of the plan. Simple plans are easier to execute, and execution is the key. Recall the equation in my "How?" graphic from a chapter ago: Inspiration + Execution = Results. Inspiration without execution (inspiration + nothing) is still only inspiration. And accurate execution requires a road map or instruction guide to what steps should be taken, who should take them, where they should be taken, how they should be taken, and when they should be completed.

In the end, you have to also be able to measure your results in order to ascertain whether your mission was successful. For years I traveled around the country stumping for IT departments to have service-level agreements (SLAs) in place with the entities they supported. Otherwise, how could IT efforts be measured? How would help-desk staffers know if they were performing well or not? After all, the only calls that they ever received had to do with things going wrong and not with things running as usual. The latter was simply expected.

Knowing how well I am doing is important because I always want to do a great job and keep improving all the time. In sales, measurement is easy; either you are making your number or not.

The number may be unrealistic, but it can be adjusted as needed. In other areas, SLAs, satisfaction or rating surveys, or some other means of measuring results need to be in place.

I have a quite simple process that I use for planning; it contains the following steps:

(Locate your Target [Rush])

1. Mission definition (what I want to accomplish)
2. Situation/gap analysis (aspects of the current environment or situation, with regard to challenges and resources)
3. Goals and objectives (steps to achieve the mission)
4. Strategies (steps to meet the goals and objectives)

(Drop your Bomb [Rush])

5. Tactics and action items (who will achieve which strategic initiatives when)

(Get Home [Rush])

6. Metrics or measurement (criteria for evaluating success levels)

Another simple way of proceeding with planning is to determine goals with the acronym MAP in mind. MAP stands for measurable, attainable, and profitable. If stated goals do not meet these criteria, it's unlikely that they can help you get to where you want to go.

Revisiting the plan quarterly, monthly, or weekly (depending on length of the mission and potential dynamics thereof) is essential in order to keep pace with change. I have been on projects where, as the deadline approached, checks were conducted and changes made even on a daily basis to successfully complete the project.

Planning is not that difficult as long as you think about your mission, think through the best way to conduct it, think about what resources will be needed to get it done, think about when the job needs to be done, and think carefully about how to determine whether you can succeed. Oh, and one last "think": think about how efficiently you can change direction if the target moves.

ACHIEVING SUCCESS DURING DISRUPTION

Attitude is the launchpad for inspiration. Positive attitude spawns positive inspiration. From that, with the right plan in place, the flow of execution will occur to move us individually and collectively in the direction of improvement and success. Without a positive attitude, you are at risk of stagnation, low motivation, and a scarcity of innovation. During highly disruptive times in a given marketplace, there's no alternative to planning to win—if survival is a goal. For example, the health-care industry today reminds me of a tempest in a teapot. Complexity, change, chaos, and confusion are a few appropriately descriptive words that portray the industry. At a recent health-care summit that I attended, the so-called plans currently being instituted by the federal government were described by policy expert Susan Dentzer from Robert Wood Johnson Foundation as "throwing as much against the wall as possible to see what will stick." During that same forum, physician and former Vermont governor and presidential candidate Howard Dean stated, "The health-care reform bill is not one I would have voted for. Those who voted didn't know what was in it."

One could easily describe this process of planning and execution as "fire, aim, ready," which is to say that adequate planning was not conducted prior to the construction of the bill, and so ongoing adjustments were required to create a more organized and thoughtful approach. The results of such an approach tend to be more dynamic than if the approach were founded on up-front planning. One might also conclude that cost overruns, missteps, and implementation challenges could be major factors throughout the process. Time will determine if this perspective is accurate. I certainly hope not, but I can't help but be reminded that "if you fail to plan, you plan to fail." The planning concept of "ready, fire, aim" is my preferred method of planning because I know that plans change, and the concept of aiming too long can be stifling to execution. I subscribe to the notion that a good plan executed and adjusted is better than a "perfect" plan that never gets implemented.

PLAN (READY)

Planning is a very important part of success. Without a plan you are prone to wander from the chosen path, to become distracted by attractive side roads, and to lose focus on your vision, mission, and target. When you plan, answer these questions:

1. Where is your view originating from? Is it in the rearview, or is it in the road ahead?
2. Do you include values, vision, and mission?
3. Are you focused on making small gains and habitually improving results and self?
4. Who do you want to become? Does it match up with where you are?
5. Are you striving for measurable, attainable, and profitable (MAP) goals?

6. Are you doing long-term, short-term, weekly, and daily planning?
7. Are you dreaming of becoming great, or are you good right where you are?

Without having the answers to these questions, you could be wandering aimlessly without direction or focus. Knowledge of the answers may not provide you with everything that you want, but it will provide you with everything you really need. Knowing that a plan is not perfect is also critical. Plans must be dynamic in nature so that change can occur within the context of your vision, mission, values, and goals.

EXECUTE (FIRE)

It is critical to execute a plan so that the results are the desired ones. The extent to which you can track success to committed goals is very important to understanding your degree of progress. Goals may change as a result of plan changes, but they shouldn't take on a life of their own outside the plan.

When executing your plan, are you

- following your inspiration or getting sidetracked?
- meeting target dates?
- meeting target quantity?
- meeting target quality?
- setting proper expectations and establishing healthy boundaries?
- building, maintaining, and executing a communication plan?
- putting a plan in place to manage inevitable change?

Establishing measurable, attainable, and profitable (MAP) goals is important to be able not only to proceed but to measure success. Not having MAP goals is like not having service-level objectives/agreements in place. How will you know how well you are doing?

REVIEW (AIM)

It is important to continuously review the success of the plan related to the goals set forth by the plan. Some important steps to take and questions to ask as you conduct your review include the following:

- Is execution occurring according to plan?
- Is the course of action taking me where I want (or need) to go?
- Is there a need, and if so, are there plans to correct the course (change)?
- Am I witnessing or experiencing continuous improvement and learning?
- Am I remaining focused on vision, values, mission, and goals?
- Do I constantly strive to keep the plan dynamic and not let it become static?

It is often very difficult to step back and look at the bigger picture during a heavily transaction-oriented day or project. Our natural human tendency is to focus only on the transaction itself so as to complete it and then move on to the next one. That is necessary work, but when it becomes the only work, you can easily lose sight of the vision, values, and mission of the project, team, company, or business. Without keeping these targets in sight, how will you know when or how to adjust your course because you are going off track? Those decisions then become instinctual—that is, driven by gut feelings, which sometimes works, but facts typically prove more effective than instincts. If I were fighting a battle in war and had a choice of either knowing exactly where over the hill the enemy was stationed or depending on my gut feeling, I would choose the facts.

Planning is a critical success factor for individuals, teams, companies, and businesses to survive and thrive. Adequate and thoughtful planning is important, but overplanning can impair the execution process. You have all heard and likely been either a victim of or the offender in "paralysis by analysis." "Ready, fire, aim" often carries a negative stigma. But in the context of building a solid plan (and recognizing that it could change due to environmental shifts), putting that plan to work for us, and then adjusting as needed, "ready, fire, aim" is the way to win the battles that will move us toward success in a disrupted situation.

As sales professionals, we are confronted regularly with change. We are also constantly trying to balance what we do with when we do it and how we do it. Handling these disruptive forces effectively requires thoughtful planning. I for one try to integrate my personal and professional lives as much as possible. If they are not properly aligned, I find myself in two separate worlds with two potentially different sets of goals and aspirations. If that ever happens to you as it has to me, ask yourself the question: how can I be optimally effectively at both?

Planning your day, your week, your quarter, your year, and your long term are all very important. They provide an integration path and a guidance system to help lead you to who you want to become, where you want to go, and what you want to do.

Passion

A critical intangible that is absolutely imperative in reaching greatness is passion. Without passion, there can be no inspiration. Passion can lead sales professionals to want to master the science of selling, the art of selling, or just the secret of success. We can be motivated by one of those factors or by an outside factor such as making money, buying a new home or car, making the Sales-Achievement Club, or taking a vacation to Hawaii. My passion for sales is about being that partner that my clients depend on to help them be successful. If they can become that comfortable and confident with me, there is little chance that I will do anything to let them down.

Regardless of what you think of what happened in the years following his many victories, do you believe that Lance Armstrong was passionate about winning the Tour de France? I do! Armstrong was stricken with cancer and had tremendous obstacles to surmount in order to become the person many believed to be the greatest athlete of all time. He was truly blessed by his recovery from cancer and of course had some outstanding physical capability, but his internal drive was what put him over the top.

Do you think that Erik Weihenmayer, the first blind man to climb Mount Everest, was passionate? I know he was! I know someone who has hiked with this character of a man, and I have heard the man who led him to the top of Mount Everest tell the story. Erik could have accepted the typical life of a blind man, but instead he stepped out (and continues to step out) of his comfort zone far more than the vast majority of us. As a result, he has received great rewards—and awards!

Paralympic summer and winter gold-medal winner Alana Nichols is another example of an "overcomer" with great passion for life and doing her best at whatever she undertakes. She helped lead the US women's wheelchair-basketball team to a gold medal and has won multiple gold medals on her monoski in Alpine events. She gets strapped into a "bucket" atop that single ski and flies down a mountain with seemingly reckless abandon, reaching speeds of sixty-five to seventy miles per hour. It takes not only great courage but also great passion for Alana to do what she does. After a near-death snowboarding crash at the age of seventeen that left her paralyzed from the waist down for the remainder of her life, Alana could have easily taken on a victim role, given up, and become just another face in a crowd. But something inside her, as she tells the story, didn't permit her to fall into drugs, alcohol abuse, and a life stripped of athletics. Months and years of rehabilitation and learning to live a brand-new life in a wheelchair somehow inspired her to reinvent herself and do whatever she could to make something special of her life. She is not only an incredibly successful athlete, but also an outstanding inspirational speaker. Instead of fading away, she is shining a light into the world as few of us ever will. Alana's story is even more remarkable than it appears on the star-studded surface. The impact that this one beautiful life is having motivates so many to reach for more and be encouraged to make the best of their situation, regardless of where they find themselves. Alana's passion is truly contagious.

On a much lesser scale, I personally was passionate about leaving my family-of-origin lifestyle behind and stepping out into the world to be someone other than who I had been. I learned at a fairly young age that taking risks was important to me. I learned how to grab hold of opportunities without trying to second-guess their outcomes. Another favorite expression of mine that applies to this line of thinking is "If I don't know where I am going, I can't ever be lost." It means that by not always trying to control outcomes—or even considering what might happen at all—I become capable of taking risks. I don't try to realize a particular form of success necessarily; I just always know that I want something special to happen. That attitude helps cushion the fall when I fail. It is similar to doing the right thing regardless of potential repercussions. For most of my life, doing the right thing regardless of the consequences has really frightened me. But some do it because it is the right thing to do, and they really want to do the right thing. While they may also be afraid, they do the right thing anyway and trust that the outcome will be favorable. There is something incredibly liberating in that thought. In recent times it became more and more important to me and now is a very comfortable part of my reality. Fear of failing and thus becoming what I often refer to as "unlovable" because of failure is not the obstacle to risk taking that it once was. Over time it becomes less and less a factor that holds me back from going after my best.

Take a few short moments to ask yourself the following questions and then consider the what-ifs of both positive and negative responses:

1. How passionate are you?
2. Do you think it shows?
3. Do you associate with other people who are passionate about their work, about their goals, and about their continuous improvement?
4. Do you believe that passion is the first step to achievement?

Whether positive or negative answers were given to these questions, think for a moment about change, cost, benefit, and whether or not you want to take that first all-important step. You may want to write down your answers to these questions and refer to them often (perhaps daily) when setting your goals. Then go ahead and do what you think is best for your success. I'll bet you will be glad that you did.

Passion for what you are becoming and doing is the icing on the cake. Without it, the cake will never be a party favorite.

The Silver Bullet

Selling through leadership is not a "silver bullet" that you can pull out of your shirt pocket, as Barney Fife used to do on *The Andy Griffith Show*. It cannot assure you of hitting the target—that is, closing a deal—each and every time you shoot. Selling through leadership is a mind-set and a heart-set that requires a special spirit within you to desire something different, unique, and very valuable in your relationship with your prospects, your clients, your teammates, and your partners. It is a way of thinking and acting that makes the ordinary, extraordinary. It stems from inspiration followed by a commitment to rely on the concept as a driving force, stick with it for a lifetime, and strive to get better at it every minute of every day. Selling through leadership requires the commitment that Vince Lombardi referred to when he said, "Perfection is not attainable, but if we chase perfection we can catch excellence." Those who have that spirit within them must commit to a lifetime of focus, improvement, self-denial, and service to others to help them succeed.

Several years ago I contemplated leaving sales and pursuing a technical-vocational path. I had developed a negative mind-set about selling, which had become an uncomfortable struggle for me. I had a reasonably good technical background and some solid management experience, so I thought that I could be successful without having to carry that ugly sales bag any longer. I was searching for my professional purpose and a vision that would guide me along a reasonable career path.

Fortunately, that negative mind-set regarding sales was a temporary one, and I rediscovered the magnificent world of selling. In that world I can compete hard and enjoy winning as well as lose and learn from failures. I can turn obstacles into opportunities. I can be an individual and at the same time part of a very special team.

In the end, however, what has become really important for me is that I am helping others to succeed and realize their own unique potentials. Often I am doing so in small ways, through little things, but I am always engaged. I may be offering some encouraging words to a teammate. I may be holding a teammate to his or her best because I care enough about the teammate to do so. I may be providing sage counsel to a customer, such as a solution for a challenge the customer is facing, or some quick service or a good price on a simple, low-cost product. That is my "silver bullet."

As I have often stated, "Everyone sells, whether they want to admit it or not. Selling encompasses all of life and occurs in every aspect of living. When performed in the context of helping others, selling is a most honorable and rewarding profession."